D0881251

SEEK MY FACE, SPEAK MY NAME

SEEK MY FACE, SPEAK MY NAME:

A Contemporary Jewish Theology

Arthur Green

JASON ARONSON INC.
Northvale, New Jersey
London

Production Editors: Judith D. Cohen and Gloria L. Jordan
Editorial Director: Muriel Jorgensen
Calligraphed Hebrew letters by Peggy M. Davis

This book was set in 12 point CG Bem by Lind Graphics of Upper Saddle River, New Jersey, and printed and bound by Haddon Craftsmen of Scranton, Pennsylvania
.

Library of Congress Cataloging-in-Publication Data

Green, Arthur, 1941–
    Seek my face, speak my name : a contemporary Jewish theology /
Arthur Green.
        p.   cm.
    Includes bibliographical references and index.
    ISBN 0-87668-592-0
    1. Judaism—Essence, genius, nature.   2. Judaism—Doctrines.
3. Mysticism—Judaism.   I. Title.
BM565.G68   1992
296.3—dc20   91-23082

Manufactured in the United States of America. Jason Aronson Inc. offers books and cassettes. For information and catalog write to Jason Aronson Inc., 230 Livingston Street, Northvale, New Jersey 07647.

למען אחי ורעי

Havurat Shalom, 1968–1973
Germantown Minyan, 1975–
Reconstructionist Rabbinical College, 1984–
and in loving memory of
Daniel Kamesar תנצב"ה

סברי חברי

CONTENTS

CREATION   49

REVELATION   99

ACKNOWLEDGMENTS

As this manuscript reaches completion, I am filled with gratitude to החונן לאדם דעת. There is much here that I did not know that I thought or understood until I started to say it. I take responsibility for all of it, but credit for very little.

My wife, Kathy, has been a firm but gentle critic throughout this work. I thank her for her prodding and her reluctance to be easily satisfied. Our daughter, Hannah Leah, also paid a price for the writing of this book, exacted mostly in precious hours of family time. I hope that she will appreciate her contribution to it, as I do.

First drafts of the chapters of this book were offered as a lecture series at New York's West End Synagogue in 1988. I thank the members of that congregation for their encouragement.

Several friends have read one or more chapters while the work was in process. I am grateful to Seth Brody, Jonathan Chipman, Everett and Mary Gendler, Barry Holtz, Rivka Horwitz, and Joseph and Gail Riemer for their insightful comments. I also read chapters to my students and to colleagues in the Reconstructionist Rabbinical Association. I am grateful to more individuals in those groups than I can list.

My secretary at RRC, Evelyn Gechman, worked with me through the many versions of this manuscript, most of which arrived on her desk alongside a full complement of college correspondence and other work. I am especially grateful for her enthusiasm in getting back to the manuscript whenever a moment was to be found.

The dedication of this volume speaks for itself. These chapters result from many conversations, teaching sessions, and *divrey torah* over these twenty-some years. I feel myself to be one who has been much blessed, both by teachers and good friends. But in looking back over these decades, I have no hesitation at all in saying מתלמידי יותר מכולם, "from my students I learned most of all."

INTRODUCTION

Once there was a king. That king had a wise man who
was his closest advisor. One day he called the wise
man into his chambers and said to him:

"You see that here in my palace I have a collection of
portraits of all the kings of all the countries. But there is one
king of whom I have no portrait and, in fact, no one has a
portrait of him. He designates himself as 'a mighty hero, a man
of truth, and a humble person.' As far as might is concerned, I
know that he is indeed powerful since he lives in a country
surrounded by the sea. On that sea there stands a fleet of ships
equipped with cannons and they do not let anyone approach
the country. If anyone should get beyond the ships, the whole
country is surrounded by a great swamp. Through that
swamp there is only a single path. That path is so narrow that
only one man could walk it at a time, and there too there are

cannons. If someone comes to fight them, they shoot those cannons and it is impossible to approach. So I know that he is indeed powerful. But how he could designate himself 'a man of truth and a humble person'—this I do not know. That king is hidden from people. He sits behind a curtain and remains distant even from his subjects. I want you to go and fetch me a portrait of that king."

The wise man went to that country. But before he went there, he knew that he had to know the essence or the secret of that country. How could he get to know it? Only by knowing how to laugh at the country. When you want to really know something, you have to know how to laugh at it.

At the center of all the countries of the world there stands a certain country. That country includes all other countries within it. Within that country there is one city, and that city contains within it all the cities of all the countries of the world. Within that city there is a single house that contains within it all the houses of all the cities of all the countries in the world. Within that house there lives one man, and he contains within himself all the people in all the houses of all the cities in all the countries in the world. And that man laughs at the entire world.

So the wise man took some money with him for the journey and went to that place at the center. He saw that there they were performing all kinds of jests and jokes about the country he sought and he came to understand through those jokes that the place he sought was the country of lies. It was filled with lies from beginning to end.

Armed with this knowledge, he went to that country. As soon as he got there, he went to the marketplace and there he let himself be cheated. Sure enough, the merchant deceived him. When he tried to call a policeman, he was cheated again. He went before the magistrate and again was cheated. When he went to trial he saw that the entire system was filled with lies and bribery. Then he tried to give a bribe himself, and the officials took the bribe, but on the very next day they did not recognize him. He went on to a higher court, and there too everything was filled with lies and bribery. Then he came before the senate, and it was just the same as all the others. Finally, he was brought before the king.

When the wise man came before the king, he cried out: "Over whom are you king? Whom do you rule? Your whole country is one big lie; it is filled with lies from beginning to end! There is not a bit of truth in it!" And he began telling the king about all the lies of the country.

The king, who was hidden behind his curtain, bent his ears forward toward the curtain to hear the wise man's words. He was amazed to know that there was someone here who knew all about the lies of his country. The ministers of the kingdom, hearing the wise man's words, were very angry. But they could not stop him, for the king had already begun to listen.

Then the wise man concluded: "Now you might say that the king of the country of lies is himself the greatest liar of them all. For who could rule the kingdom of deceit if not the greatest liar! But now I see how you are indeed 'a man of truth.' You are far from these lies and you cannot stand to look upon them. It is for this reason that you dwell behind a curtain. You are a man of truth who cannot bear to look upon the lies of your kingdom."

And so the wise man began praising the king more and more, heaping praises upon him. But the king was very humble, and his true greatness lay in his humility. So it is with humble people: the more you praise them, the smaller they feel in their own eyes. The wise man, on his side of the curtain, kept praising the king more and more, building him up higher and higher. The king, behind the curtain, being a truly humble person, began to feel smaller and smaller. The more the wise man built him up, the smaller and more humbled he felt until

xvi   INTRODUCTION

the moment when he finally became so small that he was
nothing at all. At that moment the king could no longer
restrain himself and he cast aside the curtain, saying: "Who is
this that knows all the lies of my kingdom and reveals them
all?"

   In that moment the face of the king was revealed. The wise
man saw him, painted his portrait, and took it home to his
king.

This tale by Rabbi Nahman of Bratslav has become my story.
I have been retelling it for twenty years or more. Whenever I
tell the tale, I ask those who are hearing it for the first time to
share with me in the task of interpretation. Seldom do I tell it
without coming away with some new meaning that I had
never seen in the story before.

   Why has this tale fascinated me for so many years? I see
myself as a seeker, like its hero and its author. I am engaged in
a quest for understanding and awareness, an ongoing quest to
know. As is the way of such journeys, its origins are quite
obscure. Personal journeys seldom have a clear beginning,
and they rarely have a definite end. If there is an end to our
journey, surely it is one that leads to some measure of wisdom,
and thence back to its own beginning. But somewhere along
the way, we come to realize that we know where we have
been going, why we have been going. Most of all, we come to
understand as best we can the One who sends us on our way.

   The tale is especially attractive because of its ambiguity.
There is something wrong with the story, or at least so it
appears on the surface. This is a Jewish story about a king, and
everybody knows that in Jewish stories the king is always
God. But there are two kings here—the king who is discovered at the end of the tale and the king who sends the wise man

on his way in the first place. Which of them is God, and who is the other? Or could they both be God, and how then does the story work? What is it that the wise man sees as the curtain is cast aside at the end of the tale? Is it the king? The One he knew all along, or a new King? Is it God, the eternal Other, or is it perhaps himself? Or does the tale's ambiguity hint that these lines should not be drawn so firmly? And what of the king—may the same questions not be asked of him? What does he see when the curtain is put aside? What is it that he learns about his kingdom? What does the original king gain in having this new portrait? How does it differ from all the others?

The tale is one of those rare and wonderful places where Judaism's dualistic language transcends itself, where the two or the many turn out to be one after all. The reader first thinks there must be two kings, one at the beginning and one at the end. As we begin to think about the tale, however, the two turn out indeed to be one. It is a new and unique portrait of himself that the original king demands of the seeker. But once the two kings turn out to be one, we are forced to ask whether king and seeker are not also separate aspects of the same self. When the curtain is thrown aside, what is it that both king and seeker see? Is it not the human being, made "in the image and likeness of God" that the king sees? And is it not that very image and likeness that is revealed to the seeker? Do not both king and seeker see in that moment that their otherness is not so "other" after all?

But enough of commentary and questions. In a certain sense, this entire book may be read as a comment on the tale and a series of thoughts that come from two or three decades of living with it.

Theology, more than most other forms of writing, is a

highly personal affair. It requires both an "I" and a "we." While the theologian attempts to articulate a "we," to give expression to a world view that he or she hopes the religious community might share, underlying this "we" there is always an "I." Any theological statement is in fact a sharing with others of its author's experience of his or her life in the world, an attempt to articulate that experience through the language and symbols of a community's shared religious tradition. Especially for us as Jews, theology can only exist in the context of community. In the broadest sense, this is the covenanted Community of Israel, a people that shares destiny, language, and faith. In the more narrow sense it is *havurah,* a fellowship circle of those who can both talk and pray with one another. Each such circle exists within other circles, both concentric and overlapping, until they reach out and embrace the entire House of Israel, and perhaps even further. In writing a book of theology, I invite the reader to join into my extended *havurah* circle, to be part of the community of people with whom I can share such words.

This invitation is an open and sincere one. I could hardly have written this book without having such an invitation in mind. At the same time, I recognize that not all readers will feel equally comfortable as they join into this circle. The book is addressed primarily to Jews, and the non-Jewish reader may feel left out of the shared symbolism that forms the very structure of this work. I regret this inevitable distance between us, but I repeat my welcome and I urge such a reader to persevere. In a different way, some Jewish readers may feel themselves distant from the tone of this book, either because of its extensive use of the mystical tradition or its rather unusual combination of seeming piety and frank unorthodoxy. I have always enjoyed defying categorization, though my sympathies go out to the reader who does not know what to make of the Jew who writes these words.

I am also very much aware that the "I" who speaks here is a man and not a woman. In an age when women speak quite freely about their experiences of being female, I find myself, in reflecting upon what I have written here, fully ready to say that this is an account of one contemporary man's life and the Judaism that proceeds from it. My identity as a male is in no way separable from my experience of life as a person, as a Jew, as a late twentieth-century American, and all the rest. The "we" that is here offered to the reader is given hopefully without any diminution of my own "I." To do so would in fact undercut the very meaning of this book. Each unique portrait is needed by the king.

Theology is also an attempt to articulate that intangible we call "religious experience." It seeks to use the best of human thinking and the deep reservoir of religious symbols to create a framework within which we can understand this vital and currently much-neglected aspect of human life. Religious experience is the starting-place of all theology, the most basic datum with which the theologian has to work.

What is the nature of this experience? It is as varied as the number of individual humans that there are in the world, and potentially as multiple as there are moments in each of those human lives. In the midst of life—perhaps in a great moment of confrontation with birth or death, in seeing great beauties of nature, in love and sharing with another, or in profound aloneness—but sometimes without any apparent provocation at all—a moment of holy and awesome presence comes upon us. It may come as a deep inner stillness, quieting all the sound that usually fills our inner chambers, or as a rush and excitement that fills us to overflowing. It may seem to come from within or from without—or perhaps from both at once. For some it may be evoked by music, or by awe before a great work of art. For others—far too few—it is evoked in a place of worship. We open our eyes, as it were, after such a moment, and that which we see or hear or know may be just a bit more intense and more "real" than it was before. Life has become more animated; it seems that an extra measure of energy has flowed into the scene before us. The world is the same world, but we see it with renewed vision. The vision moves us to pray: "Blessed are You, Y-H-W-H our God, eternal hidden ruler, who opens the eyes of the blind." Thanks to the One who has opened our eyes once again, who has allowed us to see.

Such moments tell us that the natural world itself may be a source of endless wonderment, unfathomable beauty, inexplicable but overwhelming joy. This realization fills us with a sense of magnificence, of smallness, and of belonging, all at once. Our heart fills with love for the world around us and with awe before its grandeur. Nothing spectacular needs to happen in order for us to be overwhelmed by the sense of an ineffable presence that fills the universe and binds us to it. We have only to be present, to be open to the miraculous bounty of life that ever surrounds us. Life reveals itself to us in all its unity and fullness. At such times we affirm with the prophet that "the whole earth is filled with God's glory."

I speak here of a certain wondrous quality of life, perhaps something well perceived in childhood and grasped by us adults only in moments of inspiration. I recognize that the quality of which I speak lies somewhere between a claim for the natural world itself and one of appreciation of our ability to be uplifted by it. Is the process of conception and birth, or that of the annual cycle of nature as seen in the budding, flowering, and fall of trees, for example, miraculous and wondrous in *itself,* or only in the *response* it calls forth in us? I look out, as I walk down a roadway in early summer, at the infinitely varied shadings of green in field and forest. Do the beauty and fullness of heart I feel reside in the miracle of the great colors with which the world has been drawn, or is it rather the miracle of the human heart and the sensitivity of our response to that particular range of colors by which we are surrounded so much of the time? Surely it feels that the process of conception and birth, the annual cycle of nature, and all the rest are themselves somehow wondrous, not just our reaction to them. But I fully recognize that this feeling is our own, inseparable from the mental–emotional responses of the human self. When speaking of the Divine presence or majesty in these, I speak of a wonder that is in no way separable from our own *sense* of wonder.

It is individual experiences like these, appreciations of wonders in nature or in the human soul, that cause us to turn inward. We seek within our own inner depths the threads of a fabric that will allow us to draw such isolated experiences together. Returning from such a moment of illumination, our hearts long to pray. The fullness we feel in such a moment seeks to break forth in thanksgiving, reaching out to the mystery that has touched us, in gratitude for our joy. At the very same time, we realize that such moments remain fleeting in our lives, and our hearts well up with longing: How can I remain faithful to such a high point of insight? How will I get back to it once I have returned to my "normal" way of being? How can I construct a life that leaves room for such moments?

All this is the stuff of prayer, in which we find room for both the fullness and the longing. But how do we pray? In what words? In what language? Where are the words powerful enough to contain the fullness of the human heart? How do we sing to the universe of our joy and cry out to it in our longing? These questions joined together create the search for a religious language. They are the threads out of which the broad tapestry of spiritual life will eventually be woven.

It is in the course of our search that we turn to the wisdom and language of religious tradition. Initially, we may be less convinced by the "truth-claims" of tradition than we are powerfully attracted to the richness of its language, both in word and in symbolic gesture. Through the profound echo chamber of the countless generations of its faithful, it offers us a way to express both the longings and the fullness that we know within. The language of sacred tradition, shrouded in mystery and awe, comes to seem like the appropriate vehicle through which to express those same feelings with regard to life itself. True, the words are antiquated, grandiose, and clearly far from anything we would choose to say if we were making up a language of our own. But precisely because the language of tradition so reaches into antiquity and is enriched by the lives of all those generations that have lived within it, it has a depth that words of our own simply cannot reach.

Cautiously, hesitantly, I begin to make the words of tradition once again my own. I hesitate because I know that its story is not quite my story, that it will try to take me along on its journey as I seek to appropriate it in order to express mine.

Ultimately, we will strike a bargain, the tradition and the seeker. I will enter into its language, celebrate the weekly recreation of the world, the liberation from bondage in Egypt, the standing before the mountain to hear God's word. I will do so not as a literal "believer," but rather as one who recognizes that all these "events" are themselves metaphors for a truth whose depth reaches far beyond them.

I know that religious language is not just a collection of stories, but an attempt to put into narrative form a truth so profound that it cannot be told except when dressed in the garb of narration. This particular narration, that of my people, I make my own. I surrender to its power and allow myself to become another link in the chain of generations. What I ask in return is only that the ongoing process of tradition not be seen as closed. I plead—a plea addressed to God, to history, or perhaps to myself—that my generation too might add its hand to the shaping of that which will be seen as tradition by those who come after us.

Religion begins not with doctrine, not with tradition, but with the need to pray. Theology comes only later, the mind's reflection on what the heart already knows. But what is the relationship between that emotional need to pray, to express the heart's fullness and longing, and all the claims of religion that still seem so distant? Is vague spiritual longing the same as religious truth? Where is the bridge that leads us over the chasm that lies between them?

We no longer react to the sense of wonder and beauty in creation like the medieval philosopher, who could derive from nature the logical conclusion that the world must indeed have been made by a great and carefully planning creator. We have no logical inference here, but only ongoing intuition.

That intuition is guided by a critical choice we have made, the choice to speak religious language. The step from "wonder" to "God" is not an act of inference, but an act of *naming*. In saying "God" in prayer, I give the object of my wonder a *name*. It is I, or we as a community, who have performed that act of naming. It is we who attach the word "God" to our search for meaning, to our desire to find a word for that which evokes our sense of awe and wonder, for that which humbles and inspires us, for that which calls us to its service.

Our quest is not a question, one in need of a specific *answer*. But the quest itself leads us to an act of *affirmation*. There is a point in our search where we say "Yes!" This is the only answer we need, and it comes forth from our own inner depths. The move from quest to affirmation may come gradually, may even seem to sneak up on us and catch us unawares. That "yes" is an affirmation of the questing process, but even more, it is an affirmation of life itself. It is the permission we give ourselves to call upon the name of God, to open ourselves to life in this deeply personal way. Within our prayers we have found a living presence, a reality beyond words. Without breaking our inner silence in any way, it has said to us: "I am." We respond with the wholeness of our being: "You, Holy One, dwell amid the prayers of Israel." All this is contained within our silent "Yes!"

We recognize that our religious language is not the only one in which the reality we encounter could be captured or celebrated. We choose, in response to that very real encounter, to invoke the name of God. But we also remain aware that it is we—as contemporary seekers and as a traditional civilization—who perform that act of choosing and naming. I believe that this act, this turn from quest to affirmation, from appreciation of wonder to calling it by God's name, is the most ennobling and significant of human speech-acts. It is the turning point in the path, the new beginning of the quest. It is one of those places, in this great circular journey back to origins, where beginning and end are joined together.

With this we are ready to begin.

GOD AND THE WAYS OF BEING

THE SECRET OF THE *SH'MA*

At the center of worship stands a cry. This cry itself is beyond worship, almost beyond words. All of our prayers, the ordered literary creation of our best rabbinic minds, serve as mere accompaniment to this cry. They prepare us for it, lead us up to the appropriate moment, coax the cry forth from deep within us, and then gently guide us back from it.

The cry itself—*Sh'ma Yisra'el*—"Hear O Israel, Y-H-W-H our God, Y-H-W-H is One!"—is not addressed to God. It is a call to Israel, to ourselves, and to those around us. It is a call to all who struggle with the divine and the human, who struggle to understand. It is our cry to one another; we call it out as the angels call out "Holy, holy, holy!" This act of calling demands all our strength; sometimes it even demands life itself. It is the act for which the term *kavvanah*, or inner direction, seems to have been made.

The call is followed by a whispered response: "Blessed is the name of God's glorious kingdom forever and ever!" The whispered silence of that response—as though it were some great secret—is broken only on Yom Kippur. On that day alone we dare to recite the response aloud. The character of that day is in fact transformed by this crucial change in the liturgy. It is the day on which we feel ourselves sufficiently holy to proclaim aloud that this world is God's kingdom, or that earth itself is the realm of Y-H-W-H.

This book may be read as an inquiry into that cry. It is an attempt to probe deeply into oneness, to seek the meaning of *Sh'ma Yisra'el* and its place in our religious lives as Jews. It seeks an understanding of why the proclamation that God is One has such a central role in our lives—the first prayer we learn in childhood, the last words we speak before we die. It attempts to seek out the nature of the great Oneness that lies both within and beyond, the One that is not followed by any two, the One that knows no other.

שמע ישראל ה׳ אלהינו ה׳ אחד

"Hear O Israel, Y-H-W-H our God, Y-H-W-H is One!" This is the higher unity, the inner gate of oneness. According to the unity of the *Sh'ma,* all is one as though there were no many. Nothing but the One exists. God after creation and God before creation are one and the same. "You are the One until the creation of the world and You are the One since the creation of the world"—unchanged, unaffected. The world makes no difference. Its existence is wholly unreal or totally inconsequential from the point of view of the One. Infinity goes on as though our world, with all its variety and beauty, with all its suffering and crises, makes not the slightest bit of difference. The garbing of divine energy in the countless forms of existence is naught when seen from the point of view of infinity. There, only the One is real. All else, all variation, all distinction, all separateness, are but illusion. We recite this *Sh'ma* at death as we say it in life, as though to say that our death—and our life—have made no significant ripple in the great ocean of the cosmic One. Only infinity is real here: God of endless cosmic space–time.

ברוך שם כבוד מלכותו לעולם ועד

"Blessed is the name of God's glorious kingdom for ever and ever!" This is the lower unity, the outer gate, the one *within* the many. We refer to it as the unity of God's kingdom. Here we encounter God's oneness *in* and *through* the world, not despite it. Each flower, each blade of grass, each human soul, is a new manifestation of divinity, a new unfolding of the cosmic One that ever reveals itself through its multicolored garments, ever taking on new and changing forms of life. In the very variety of life's riches we discover the unity that flows through them all, the divine life that animates all of being. Here the power and oneness of God are manifest in each of the lowliest and simplest forms of being, including the inanimate, as well as they are in the most magnificent and complex creations of the human mind. Each of them, real and distinctive in itself, bears witness to the single force of being that animates and unites them all. Existence here is celebrated in variety, in specificity, rather than in vast sameness. This God too represents infinity, but the infinity of One-in-many. "The whole *earth* is filled with God's glory."

Life is about these two truths. We realize that all around us, all we do, even our own lives themselves, are emptiness and vanity, that everything but the ultimate One is mere illusion. At the same time, we know that each moment in our lives and every person and object we encounter exists through the One, as a bearer of its presence. These two truths stand in dialectical relation to one another; they represent the same finely wrought transparent vessel, here seen in emptiness, here in fullness. Our religious task is to see through to the oneness of these two truths, to recognize that the one beyond and the one within are the same One. We are then charged to create a human community that lives and witnesses an ongoing response to that insight. This is what it means to be a Jew. Nothing less.

We cannot reach the inner gate of understanding the eternal and unchanging One unless we go through the outer gate of discovering and embracing the divine presence as it fills this world. The way to God is *through* the world, not around it. It is in encountering the richness and diversity of life, in loving both people and the natural world for who and what they are, that we come to know the One. Religious experience is largely the experience of immanence, of the divine as dressed in the garments of this world. We discover the godly in the natural, through our own sense of awe and wonder. It is this experience of immanence that leads us to intuitive intimations that there is something "beyond" as well. The discovery of God begins with the sense of wonder in our encounter with the natural world that lifts it entirely out of the ordinary.

But if the worldly presence of the One is the outer gate, the one through which we must enter first, why is *Barukh Shem* to be recited in a whisper? It would seem that immanence is the less secret part of the *Sh'ma's* message—why do we keep it hidden every day but one?

Here we begin to understand both the power of the language of Oneness and the fears it arouses in us. We seek a religious language that goes beyond the separation between "God," "world," and "self," that seems so ultimate in most of Western theology. The God of which we speak here is not the "wholly other," so widely familiar in our thought and yet so little tested by real understanding. We refer rather to a deity that embraces all of being, a single One that contains within it all the variety and richness of life, yet is also the Oneness that transcends and surpasses all. Some Jewish sources speak of the transcendent and immanent aspects of the deity as *sovev*—that which "surrounds" all the worlds—and *memale*—that which "fills" all the worlds—at once. These two aspects of the divine life-flow play out an eternal dance through the history of life and through the vehicle of human consciousness. The ultimate goal, both of consciousness and of the cosmic process itself, is to reaffirm their oneness.

But such unitive thoughts are both demanding and frightening. If all is One, then each of us is not *really* a separate being. "Self" becomes something of an illusion. Our most basic understanding of who we are is called into question. The greatest masters of Jewish prayer knew this to be precisely the case. They also understood that we spend most of our lives in flight from such insights. The acceptance of Oneness means that each of us is but a part of a greater whole, a specification of the unity that embraces us.

How do we live with such a thought? Is not all of our thinking—at least in the West—based on an acceptance of individual self-consciousness as essential reality? What will it mean for us to come to terms with a vision that sees each mind as but another reflection back of Mind, each life as another "portrait of the king"? How much safer it is to retreat to the religious language of our childhood, one in which lines are clearly drawn, one in which God is clearly "up there" and I am "down here." But where do we allow room for the truth that all is One if our religious language is that of "Self" and "Other"? No wonder the claim that *this* world is God's kingdom has to be kept to a whisper! The real meaning behind that phrase is that *all* is God, that king and kingdom are one and the same. The immanence of *Barukh Shem* is more radical in its demand than is the transcendence of *Sh'ma Yisra'el*. *Sh'ma* alone might leave us to live with the illusion that God the One is still somehow the Other. *Barukh Shem* makes it clear that we too exist only as part of that Oneness.

GOD ABOVE, GOD WITHIN

The particular ancient Near Eastern culture out of which the Jewish people and our religion emerged was one that worshipped sky gods. Especially after the Bible eliminated polytheism with its pantheon of gods and concentrated all the deities and their powers into one, the primary residence of God *in the heavens* was firmly established. From its very earliest origins, Jewish (hence also Christian, Islamic, and general Western) conceptions of God were tied to this *vertical metaphor* for the God–world relationship. "Where does God live?" the child is asked. "Up there," is the answer expected of the 3-year-old, with a finger pointed toward the heavens. True, we also hope he or she will sweep a hand around and say "Everywhere!" and eventually (though probably quite a few years later) point inward to the heart as well. But the first answer expected is that which reconfirms for yet another generation the myth of verticality, the root-metaphor of our Western understanding of the relationship between God and world.

As much as we outgrow such thinking in our strivings for mature religion, the image of "God above" never quite leaves us. It is reinforced every time we read a Psalm about God who "dwells in heaven," every time we tell a story about Moses "going up to heaven" to receive the Torah, every time we encounter a text that speaks of spiritual growth as a series of "steps" up the cosmic "ladder." Even our mystical literature is much influenced by this deep-seated way of thinking: the

visionary "ascends" through the seven heavens before seeing
the throne of God's glory; the contemplative binds rung to
rung in the attempt to reach ever greater "heights" of understanding.

But suppose for the moment that we allowed ourselves to
be freed from this upper world–lower world way of thinking.
Dare we imagine a Judaism less than fully wedded to this
single metaphor? Some of our greatest philosophers and mystics surely understood that this way of seeing things could
well be replaced by one that spoke in terms of "inner" and
"outer," rather than "upper" and "lower." Let us think of the
journey to God as a journey inward, where the goal is an
ultimately deep level within the self rather than the top of the
mountain or a ride in the clouds. The Torah tells us that our
earliest ancestors were diggers of wells. Let us try to reach for
the understanding that flowed as water from the depths of
Abraham's well, rather, for the moment, than the one that
came down carved in stone from the top of Moses' mountain.
This journey inward would be one that peels off layer after
layer of externals, striving ever for the inward truth, rather
than one that consists of climbing rung after rung, reaching
ever and ever higher. Spiritual growth, in this metaphor, is a
matter of uncovering new *depths* rather than attaining new
heights. Perhaps we could even try to think of Torah itself as
having been given at the deepest level of inner encounter,
rather than from the top of the highest mountain, the mountain serving as *a vertical metaphor for an inward event.*

Have we lost our Jewish souls in the course of this exercise?
I think not. In fact, we may encounter a certain renewal of
vigor in our spiritual language as we work on reading it in this
other—and by no means entirely new—way. I am not suggesting that all vertical metaphors be eradicated from Jewish

sources. This could not be done without destroying all the beauty and ancient charm that makes the language of Judaism so attractive and valuable in the first place. The metaphor needs to be preserved, but it needs to be placed in perspective. Our attempt to replace the upper with the inner as a focus of devotion helps us to see what a central place that single vertical metaphor has in our lives, in the forming of our own psyches as well as our people's religious civilization.

Prayer, our sages surely knew, is an inward act. "The Compassionate One wants the heart," the Talmud teaches. The locus of activity in human reaching for God is primarily inward, a turning of heart and mind that is attested by, but never fully subsumed within, outward deeds. The Bible's elaborate descriptions of the Tabernacle are read by Jewish authors of many later generations as outward symbols of inward states of devotion and grace, as Israel is told to "make a Tabernacle that I may dwell *within* them."

This inwardness is not only that of the person, but the shared inner self of the human heart, the human community, and the world around us. Inwardness means that the One is to be found within all beings. We find God by a turning in to ourselves, to be sure, but also in the inward experiences that we share with others. The inner sight that we develop in such moments then leads us to an ability to see the inwardness of all creatures, to come to know them as the many faces of the One.

THE TWO AND THE ONE

But once we have gone this far in experimenting with change of our root-metaphor, we need to go yet one crucial step farther. Is the inner world of religious insight, the "place" where we most know God, really a different place than the world in which we live our lives? Is spatial distance well suited as a way of explaining the relationship between the two? Is it really an "other" of which we speak when we think of the divine reality we name as God? An "other" in the sense that you are an other to me, or in the sense that objects or locations are "other" to one another? Or might it better be defined as a quality of being, another *mode* in which this same universe may be seen to exist, a different *perspective* on the world we know so well?

The quality of otherness, when attributed to the One, is indeed essential in a certain way. We need it to indicate that the divine is very much not the ordinary, that the *order of being* or *sort of reality* about which we speak when we talk of God is not the same as that which we address when we deal with other matters. But this sense of otherness is not quite the same as saying that God is "another being," a person or object who is "over there" in some quasi-spatial realm that is different from the universe. "God" and "world" are different faces of the same reality, different modes of the only Being there is.

Surely the language of dualism is deeply rooted in the Jewish experience, ranging from the Bible's "The heavens are the heavens of God and the earth has He given to the children

of men" to Martin Buber's insistence that the I–Thou relationship is the basis of all religious life. The most radical
challenge to this dualism I have seen is captured in the midrashic tale of young Abraham smashing all the idols in his
father's house but one, and attributing that destructive act to
the single remaining idol. We Jews have never internalized the
full meaning of that story. Much of Western monotheism (the
Abrahamic faith!) is precisely that: positing not a multitude of
gods to rule the world, but rather a single all-powerful extra-
mundane deity. All of the idols are reduced to one, the Midrash says, but that one remains in power.

The God of whom (and we shall speak later of why
"whom" rather than "which") I speak is of a significantly
different order. Faith in this One that is the source and core of
all, the unity that defies and transcends all separation, has long
existed within Judaism, masked within the metaphors of duality. Our age needs a clear articulation of this faith; it is time
for Jewish nondualism to emerge from hiding. It is time to
admit that the parental, royal, and pastoral metaphors we have
inherited, beloved as they are, are not adequate for describing
the relationship between God and world as we experience and
understand it. Providence, the sense of an all-powerful God
"out there" who watches over us and keeps us from harm is
not, in its simple sense, the center of faith as we know it. The
terrible course of Jewish history in our century has made this
most conventional of Western understandings of religion
impossible, even blasphemous, for us. If there is a God of
history, an independent being who shapes the historic process, such a God's indifference to human—and Jewish—suffering might lead us to cynicism or despair, but not to worship.

But still we find ourselves praying! That is an incontrovertible fact, an essential datum our theology cannot escape. Jews who know full well what happened, who understand that the pious and impious suffered one fate, that there is no divine interference in history, *still want to pray*. And it is not only dirge and supplication or a cry of protest and anger that comes out when we pray. We want to sing to the universe, to recount its beauty, to celebrate the life that goes on after all. This act of affirmation exists on an infinitely deeper plane than does the question, "Do you believe in God?"

The deeper act of worship calls for a more profound self-understanding as well. Despite what the words say, our prayer is not quite addressed to that Other who creates, commands, and saves. Our prayer is a cry and a song to life itself, called forth from our own innermost self, addressed to the wonder and mystery of life that we have dared to call again by this ancient and holy name. The language we speak remains that of monotheism: "There is no god but You." But the content with which we fill these words goes much further: "There is *naught* but You!"

The shared use of the term "God" is not without its problems. I cannot abandon this term that bears within it so much of the legacy of our faith. I also understand that any attempt to speak *of* God necessarily betrays our living faith. Theologizing requires stepping back from the encounter and describing it in terms that are inadequate, that inevitably reduce God from living reality to object of analysis. For the non-dualist, speaking *to* God is as much of a betrayal as speaking *of*. Though I insist on using the dualist language in prayer ("blessed are You . . ."), I know that I do not mean it in its simplest sense. This language is a way of addressing the One as though it were possible for me to stand outside that One in such a moment, as though there really were an "I" who could speak this way to "Thou." But if such prayer is betrayal of our deepest consciousness, it is there to keep faith with our ordinary experience as human beings: we continue on the plane of daily consciousness to see the world as separated between self and other. It can be argued that the ability to maintain this distinction—a shallow one from the mystic's viewpoint—is crucial to the maintaining of our identity and our sanity. The self who continues to live in the world of "self" and "other" needs the dualistic language of "I" and "Thou," even though it does not mirror the deepest truth we know.

GOD AS Y-H-W-H: "IS–WAS–WILL BE IS ONE!"

I further betray my faith by the use of the English word "God," rooted as it is in old Germanic paganism. I struggle with ways to replace this term in English but come up empty-handed. By "God," of course, I mean Y-H-W-H, the One of all being. This name of God is the starting point of all Jewish theology. It is to be read as an impossible construction of the verb "to be." *HaYaH*—that which was—*HoWeH*—that which is—and *YiHYeH*—that which will be—are here all forced together in a grammatically impossible conflation. *Y-H-W-H is a verb that has been artificially arrested in motion and made to function as a noun.* As soon as you try to grab hold of such a noun, it runs away from you and becomes a verb again. "Thought does not grasp you at all," as the wise have always known. Y-H-W-H as noun can be the bearer of predicates, but those too become elusive as soon as the verbal quality of the divine name reasserts itself. Try to say anything definitional about Y-H-W-H and it dashes off and becomes a verb again. This elusiveness is underscored by the fact that all the letters that make up this name served in ancient Hebrew interchangeably as consonants and as vowels. Really they are mere vowels, mere breath. There is nothing hard or defined in their sound. The name of that which is most eternal and unchanging in the universe is also that which is wiped away as readily as a passing breath.

Here we see how inadequate a translation "God" is for Y-H-W-H. If I look for another English rendition of it, I would probably come up with "is–was–will be." Since that is awkward to use (as in "Blessed are You, Is–Was–Will Be"), I am attracted to its abstraction in the term "Being." That is probably as close as English or other Western languages will allow us to get. But the identification of God and Being, with which I am partially sympathetic, has to be handled with some caution. "Being" is itself an abstraction, a *concept;* it does not represent the same flow of energy as "is–was–will be." "Being" is static; it includes no movement. Y-H-W-H is movement and stasis at once. If Y-H-W-H includes all that is, was, or will be, bearing within it past and future existence as well as present, it includes that which by definition does not currently exist. For Y-H-W-H to translate as "Being," that term would have to embrace at once all the "was" and "will be" along with the "is," which is to say a dynamic transcendence of time.

To express it differently, God is both being and becoming, noun and verb, stasis and process. *All of being is One in a single simultaneity in God, and yet God is at the same time process without end.* Here we are back to our starting point: Y-H-W-H as *Sh'ma Yisra'el* is stasis, the great transcendent oneness; Y-H-W-H as *Barukh Shem* is process, the one within the ever-changing many. God evolves as life in the universe and on the planet evolves. The divine force that resides in the molecular structure of beings, or in DNA as well as in the stars and sky, continues to grow and change along each step of the evolutionary ladder. But that same Y-H-W-H is also the eternal and unchanging One. We may depict divinity on the one hand as a configuration of spiritual molecules involved in a process of constant change, ever rearranging themselves like a cosmic kaleidoscope. But that same deity is also the great ocean in which these ripples of change mean nothing at all, and which one day will be still again.

SPEAK MY NAME

B eing, then, approaches adequacy as an English rendition of Y-H-W-H only if it leaves room for the ever-becoming side of the One as well. But there is another reason why "Being" does not quite work as a translation for Y-H-W-H. That artificially arrested verb is used in Hebrew not only as a noun but as a *proper* noun. It differs from the word *Elohim,* the generic Hebrew term for deity. Y-H-W-H is the proper *name* of God; designated as *shem ha-meforash,* the explicit name, in Hebrew. Possessing a name renders one capable of being addressed: I call upon you by your name; I can address you directly because I know your name. The Jewish religious experience at its very root claims to know the name of God. True, it dare not pronounce this name and substitutes one circumlocution after another for it. But the unpronounced breathlike word is still there, inscribed on the diadem of the ancient priest, written in the *tefillin* of the modern worshipper or in the *mezuzah* on the doorpost of the Jewish home, or spoken—via circumlocution—at the heart of all Jewish prayer.

This central aspect of ancient Jewish worship has been all but ignored by modern readings of the liturgy. The ability to call upon God's name has a quasi-magical quality about it, something that surpasses mere supplication, or that makes true supplication possible. "I will raise him up because he knows My name," the Psalmist's God says of the worshipper. "We will *pronounce Your name* and enthrone You, our God and

King," reads our daily introduction to the morning Psalms. But this potential evocation of power over the deity—for that is the soul of magic—has another side to it as well. Knowing someone's name means knowing *personally*. The one named, at least in our experience within the human interpersonal realm, steps forth from anonymity and becomes fully human. How much harder it is to do violence to another, or to dehumanize that person, once he or she has a name! To call a person by name is to recognize that person's humanity. On the less-than-human level too, we enter into relationship with an animal, declare it our pet or protected one, by the act of naming. The giving of names, say the rabbis, was Adam's first act of wisdom, even the act that made him human. It was his ability to name that convinced the angels to have special respect for this new and different creature.

This same process takes place in the core experience of prayer as well: calling out the name is the barest essential act of worship. The very fact that we avoid direct mention of the name even in prayer, lest it be degraded, points to the almost infinite reverence with which Judaism regards this act. That this name is the very core of all names, the word that includes all words within it, is borne by the message that this is a word that can never be spoken.

It is the union of these two aspects of the word Y-H-W-H that creates the unique power of Jewish theology, as well as the tension that continues to drive it. The most abstract of words, that which encompasses being and becoming within it, is also the *name* by which that ever-elusive One is called. In joining these two in a single word, Jewish faith claims an *intimacy with the abstract*. Jewish worship proclaims the ability *to bridge abstraction and intimacy in a single act of faith*. Throughout its history, Judaism has striven on the one hand for a pure, elevated, and entirely abstract notion of God, one that removes all traces of idolatry. This striving is Judaism's representation of the intellectual growth and maturation of humanity, ever seeking to elevate and purify its highest ideal. But our tradition has also recognized the need for a religious language that allows for the whole involvement of the individual and the community—emotional as well as intellectual—that makes for living faith. The insistence that both of these are one in the single name of God, the word that transcends human language and existence itself, lies at the very core of Judaism's claim. Y-H-W-H, the essence of abstraction, is also *Israel's name* for the One, the bearer of its most intimate cry.

Because Y-H-W-H is both name and abstraction, it is both dependent upon and independent of human existence. Of course, we cannot speak of Y-H-W-H existing or not existing; to ask whether "being exists" is itself a redundancy. Existence—*HaWaYaH* in Hebrew—has no meaning outside Y-H-W-H; it is a mere reversal of the letters. But it does seem appropriate, given our current picture of the universe and our rather small place within it, to ask whether Y-H-W-H will be when the human mind is no more. If indeed our sun will one day burn out and the light that allows for all of terrestrial existence will shine no more, can we say that Y-H-W-H will continue to exist "on that day"? Of course Y-H-W-H *as name* will have ceased to function, for such a category is meaningless without a namer. But will Y-H-W-H, the One within and beyond all being, still exist? Here we can only posit that which we will never know. In a sense the answer is obvious. Of course Being will still be: there are other suns, other universes than our own. They may not have life, but they still have existence. Being itself *was* before there was a human mind to know it, and *will be* afterward as well.

But because our faith joins together the abstract and the named, the question has meaning on another and more personal level. Will the consciousness that existed in each of us, a memory of the lives we led and the faith with which we struggled, somehow continue to be alive when all of us are no longer here? As long as there are human beings, we may say that the memory of each human who has lived somehow passes into the collective memory of humanity that makes for civilization. But is there a way in which human lives are preserved after death, something other than an individual afterlife, yet beyond the living in the memories of others? Is there an all-embracing memory within the One, transcending both individual mortality and linear time itself? If so, we may presume that such a memory of us all will continue to exist, even when there is no human left to remember. *Atah zokher et kol ha-mif'al* ("You remember the entire enterprise"): the cosmic One, that which has contained all mind and all minds within it, cannot be seen as devoid of mind. Surely Y-H-W-H cannot be less than that which it has contained. And since past, present, and future are one in it, naught that has been will be lost altogether. Even when there is no more process, timeless stasis will contain all that ever was.

Ve-aharey ki-khelot ha-kol, levado yimlokh nora. "And after all is ended, God alone will rule in awe." When there is nothing left, if you will, that Nothing will still be God.

Seeking God: Look First to Love

Returning now to our own world, we ask once again where we see the eternal One manifest. As we said at the outset, we can find it anywhere, wherever the eye is open, and anytime—"Today, if you listen to God's voice." Much of the initial motivation that brings us to religion is the discovery of the divine within nature. We will have occasion later to speak of the specific Jewish claim that God is also to be discovered within Torah and the process of learning. But for us humans, God is most to be discovered within the human community, in relationships with others, and in knowing ourselves. In fact, our search for God is fully bound up with our being human; our knowledge of Y-H-W-H is in no way separable from our own humanity. We come to know God through relationships with one another, opening ourselves to the divine presence as manifest in those whom we allow ourselves to love.

Because we feel the relationship with God as one of great intimacy, we cannot help but depict it in images of the sorts of human intimacy that we know best: God as our spouse, God as our parent, God as our loving friend. The process of seeking and of growing in faith requires an opening and making vulnerable of the self that usually happen to us only in the intimacy of human relations. All of these confirm that we cannot help but speak of the divine in terms of person, confusing as that designation may be when we seek to overcome religious dualism. If I think of God as person and of a relationship with that person, am I not reconfirming the very separation that I claim to want to overcome?

The matter can only be partially understood by analogy to human relationships. Life partners who know each other well and love each other deeply have surely known moments—both sexual and otherwise—where borders between self and other have broken down and a seamless flow exists between those two, who in such a moment are in fact one. The spiritual understanding of marriage that underlies such figures of speech as "my other half" goes even further, seeing the marital union as recreating a primal unity of male and female that was lost only with guilt, self-consciousness, and the expulsion (or was it perhaps our own frightened human flight?) from Eden.

This latter sense just begins to get at what I mean by our need to see God as intimate in order ultimately to see our-selves and God as one. Or, to say it more accurately, to see ourselves and God as manifestations of the same eternal unchanging-yet-becoming One. We mortals are both blessed and condemned to live in a world of separateness, one in which each ego-consciousness sees itself as individual. Our maturity and our sanity are themselves largely created by the success of this ongoing process of individuation. This is also the strength of our Western consciousness, most notable for its respect for individual variety and creativity. Yet, behind this veil of separate and often competitive or struggling indi-vidualism, lies another reality, one in which all souls are one Soul, totally open and present to one another as they come to know that the boundaries that separate them are but illusion. Most of us humans get to glimpse this reality only a few times in our lives, and most commonly with just a single other in the context of that relationship we call love. For us simply to proclaim "All is One! All is One!" running through the streets in the kinds of ecstatic outbursts that characterized Hasidism in its early days, would only land us in the asylum. And rightly so, for we would be demanding a break with ordinary consciousness so severe that it could indeed be called schizophrenic. Our tradition therefore calls upon us to go on seeing God—the One we know to be Y-H-W-H, embracing all of being—as "other," *in order that the human mind might go on being both sane and human.*

Remember the dwellers in darkness in Plato's myth of the cave? They have to be brought out into the light gradually, educated first by shadows on the cave wall, until they can become used to the light without being blinded. Here we have one of the central myths of the Western mystical tradition. According to the Hasidic masters, latter-day heirs to and reshapers of the Platonic tradition, the greatest gift God gives us is *tsimtsum* (literally, the "contraction" of God), which to them means the illusion of our separate identity. Only bit by bit and by means of careful training are we allowed to peer beyond that veil, and always in doses that will nourish rather than destroy us. The vehicle for this growth process is the projected screen-image, the shadow-play on the wall of our cave of individuation called the personal God. It is only by going through the path of personhood, ever striving toward a greater intimacy with that "other," that we can prepare ourselves to catch an authentic glimpse of true oneness. Judaism is a tradition that loves the person, that embraces the human as God's unique image in the world. *A Jewish path to oneness can only be one that leads through human intimacy.*

In God's Own Image: Seek My Face

We encounter the divine through relationship with another person. We attempt to seek out the One through images of a person, through encountering God as another "person." Both of these are made possible for us by the Bible's most remarkable assertion that the human being is created in God's image. The person—every person—is an earthly replica or small repository of the fullness of divine energy. Thus, in truly opening ourselves to the other, we inevitably open to God as well, whether or not we choose to express it in those terms. Abraham Joshua Heschel used to teach that the reason graven images are forbidden by the Torah is not that God has no image, but because God has but one image: that of every living breathing human being. You may not fashion an image of God in any medium other than that of your entire life—that is the message of the Torah. To take an inanimate object—something less than human—and attempt to fashion a god out of it—that is indeed idolatry, a lessening of the true divine image within you.

The verses in Genesis that speak of humans being fashioned in God's image and likeness, have been interpreted and reinterpreted countless times over the centuries. These words have been made to refer to intelligence, to rationality, to freedom of moral choice, to the power of imagination, and to a host of other things. All of these take the verses far afield from their original meaning. It has always seemed to me that in their simplest sense, the verses are claiming that humans somehow *look like* God, that the human form and the divine form, however we understand those phrases, have something in common. In particular, this seems to mean that the human face—every human face—is a copy or reflection of the face of God.

Our search for a Jewish way in which to speak about life as an ongoing religious quest inevitably brings us back to the Psalmist, and especially to those passages where the author of the Psalms cries out to "seek My face," "to behold the beauty of God," or "to dwell in God's courts." The quest, when put in Jewish language, is our longing for intimacy, for a "face-to-face" relationship with the Divine. We long to repeat the experience of Moses, who could converse with God "face to face, like a person with his neighbor." The most ancient and revered blessing that has been passed down among Jews from generation to generation contains the phrase "May God cause His face to shine upon you," as though to say that God is possessed of a shining or radiant countenance.

The God of our tradition has a face so radiant that when Moses comes down from the mountain after being with Y-H-W-H, his face shines so brightly that he is forced to wear a mask. An ancient poem preserved in the synagogue liturgy for Yom Kippur tells of the priest coming forth from his annual visit to the Holy of Holies, his face shining like the sun. Both prophet and priest, the two great models for religious intimacy in our ancient sources, seem to take into themselves something of God's own shining face in their moments of most intimate contact with the Divine.

We shudder, of course, at such a fully anthropomorphic concept of God. At the very least, we would follow Maimonides in understanding the "face" of these passages in a metaphoric way. God's "face" refers to God's presence, a sense of close encounter or intense awareness. If God has a face, we tend to believe, surely it is a projection of the human face. It is we who take the mysterious and faceless One of the universe and make it into a humanlike deity. That is our need and our right. God would have no face if we did not ascribe a face to God. But what face is it that we ascribe to the One? Does each of us lend to God his or her own face? Is it the multiple faces of those we love in our lifetime that we collectively project onto God? (What face is it that the wise man sees in our story?) Or is "face" only an inherited figure of speech, something that we pick up from the ancient sources of traditional religion, rather than something that we create or project on our own?

Here I am reminded of another hasidic story. A tale is told of Rabbi Nahman Kossover, a contemporary of the Ba'al Shem Tov. Reb Nahman was one of the many kabbalists who believed that the proper way for you to remain attached to God was ever to contemplate the four-letter name Y-H-W-H, and to actually see the letters of the divine name always before you. He was a preacher, and it was said that when Reb Nahman looked out at the faces of those to whom he spoke, he was able to see the letters of the divine name reflected back to him. But then times changed and the preacher was forced to become a merchant. In the marketplace, amid the rapid pace of buying and selling, he found it harder always to concentrate on the name of God. So we are told that he hired a special assistant who came with him wherever he went. That person's function was to remind him of God's name. Whenever he looked at the face of his assistant, Reb Nahman would remember the name of God.

I have been thinking about this assistant for a good many

years. I wonder what he looked like. Dare we think that he
was particularly beautiful? Probably not, given the values of
traditional Jewish society. Might he, on the other hand, have
been particularly tormented? Might it have been in the agony
of a suffering face that Reb Nahman saw the letters of the
divine name, as we might see God in the face of a Holocaust
survivor, truly echoing Job's "In my flesh I see God"? Or was
it, to be less dramatic, a face that bore what is called in Yiddish
edelkeyt, a certain combination of gentleness, warmth, and
nobility? Could it have been a face like this that somehow
reminded the master of the name—and the face—of God? My
own best guess about Reb Nahman Kossover's assistant, the
image of whom has followed me around all these years, is that
his face was quite ordinary. He was simply a human being,
another human being made in God's image. But he was there
to serve as a reminder. Reb Nahman looked at a human being,
and in the very ordinariness of that human face he remem-
bered to concentrate on the eternal, mysterious, and ineffable
name.

This most ancient understanding is preserved in the
teaching of Hillel, who claimed that keeping one's body clean
was like washing the statues of the emperor that had been put
up throughout the kingdom. It is the body, Hillel still understood, not just the mind or soul, that is in God's image. To
truly see a human being, he taught, is to see a living statue or
image of Y-H-W-H.

A nice sentiment, you may say, but still just projection. It is
we who determine that God has a face. It is by the act of saying
"thou" to the faceless cosmos that we give it a face and turn it
from object into subject, creating a projected God with whom
we may enter into dialogue and conversation. I do not dis-

agree with this claim at all. I am fully aware of the crucial role projection plays in religion and in all our images of God. But I also do not believe the matter is quite that simple. *Our need to create God, I believe, comes out of the deepest recesses of ourselves, the place within us that also knows, in a way we cannot fully articulate, that God created us.* We are but an effulgence of the One, a ray of that light called Y-H-W-H. From deep within us, there wells up a need to testify to that truth, to construct a reality that will remind us of our hidden source.

We are created in the image of God, if you will, and we are obliged to return the favor. God seeks to make us become ever more holy; we seek to make God human. The divine voice deep within each of us (and given expression within all the great human religious traditions) calls upon us to reshape our lives as embodiments of divinity. This inner drive to imitate our source calls forth in us the unceasing flow of love, generosity of spirit, and full acceptance, both of ourselves and of all God's creatures. Frightened by our own mortality and ultimate powerlessness, we cannot live with a faceless God. We will strive to mold ourselves over in the image of divinity. But in exchange we need a God to whom we can cry, with whom we can argue, whom we can trust, and even love. For us humans, such a God needs to have a human face. *So the face is our gift to God. But the light that shines forth from that face and radiates with love—that surely is God's gift to us.*

The understanding that projection plays a key role in our theological imagination, so central to the modern understanding of religion since Feuerbach, Nietzsche, and Freud, is not original to these moderns. Maimonides' claim that prophecy contained a perfect mixture of intellect and imagination already points in this direction. What is the role of imagination in religion, if not to project images from our own experience that will serve as vessels to catch and embody the light? The kabbalists refer to this insight in their distinction between *Eyn Sof,* the boundless, undefined, and essentially impersonal divine reality, and the *sefirot,* which may be seen as the multiple faces or masks of God. Their understanding of projection, however, was theologically rather complicated and profound. They saw Y-H-W-H as the totality of Being and Becoming, a fount and channel of energy without limit and without end. This stream contains all images, all symbols, all words within it. It is only our limitation as receivers of the flow that isolates certain images, filtering out the infinite number that do not fulfill our needs, and responding only to those that do. It is only from our limited point of view that we see this process as projection. Seen from God's perspective, as it were, it is the diminution of infinity so that it can enter the finite human mind.

But even before the new intellectual refinements of the Middle Ages, the rabbis knew that our images of God were projections brought about by human need. The Midrash claims that there are two great moments when Israel actually saw the divine form. At the crossing of the Red Sea, they saw God as a young lover and hero. At Sinai they saw an elderly lawgiver and judge. Each revelation was in accord with the need of the hour. In the day of battle, a frail elderly God could hardly be the right vision for the moment. On the day of judgment, no one could be satisfied with a God who looked any less distinguished than the jurists of the day, "the elders who sit at the gate." What is this midrash if not a primitive understanding of projection? A particularly startling hasidic interpretation of the Prophet Ezekiel's vision says that "the figure with the appearance of a man" that Ezekiel saw sitting on the divine throne is there only because we place him there. The mystic, who sees far beyond the figure of "God," is not afraid to admit to projection.

Another old rabbinic source, to which we have referred briefly, reflects on the origin of the important term *Adonay* ("my Lord"), used since ancient times as a replacement for the unpronounceable Y-H-W-H. When God created Adam, so the tale goes, the angels were jealous of him. The new creature was too obviously the delight of God and the object of divine affection. "What is man that thou art mindful of him," they mocked, the rabbis here putting a line from the Psalter in the angels' mouths. God decided to show the angels this new creature's wisdom. A series of animals was brought before the angelic hosts, and they were asked to name them. Having no part in this material world, they were unable to identify (or identify with) the animals. Then Adam was called forth, and he gave an appropriate name to each of the beasts. Once he had succeeded at this task, God asked: "And what is your name?" to which Adam answered: "I should be called Adam, for I was taken from *adamah*, or earth." God asked once again: "And what should I be called?" Adam answered: "You are *Adonay*, for You are Lord over all Your works."

This midrash is a recognition that *it is we humans who need to assert the lordship of God.* Y-H-W-H, the true name of the One, has nothing to do with mastery or domination. It is a name that bespeaks the utter oneness, rather than the hierarchical ordering, of existence. Only when humans enter the scene, with their own needs for both dominion and submission, does the name Y-H-W-H need to be replaced by "Lord." This is our act, a projection onto the One of the ordering found in human society.

None of this is to say, of course, that divinity is "not real," or that religion is "just made up." Quite the contrary. It is *because* religion is so real and addresses the human spirit at such great depth that we are forced to turn into ourselves and bring forth the most profound creations of the human spirit as reflecting mirrors with which to catch the divine light. All the prophets but Moses, say our sages, prophesied "through a darkened glass," which really means through a mirror. One ancient midrash says that the seeker is like a tired animal wandering through the forest who suddenly comes upon a pond. He looks down into the pond and thinks he sees another. That other is his reflection, of course, but in seeing himself projected outward in the form of another, he is allowed to see himself for the first time.

FACE TO FACE

Seeing God. The Torah itself seems to be conflicted on the question of whether such a thing can happen, or ever has happened, even at Sinai. Moses asks to see God's face and is told "No human may see Me and live." Not that there is nothing to see; the point here seems to be that the experience of seeing God is so intense and powerful that it will bring on death. When God passes by the cleft of the rock where Moses is hidden at Sinai, he is told "You will see My back, but My face may not be seen." And yet in another chapter, also describing the Sinai experience, the text says quite clearly of Moses, Aaron, and the seventy elders, "They saw the God of Israel." The book of Deuteronomy, in recounting the Sinai experience, severely warns the reader that there was no visual component to that experience, lest future generations be led into an attempt to represent that vision of God in material form. Yet, it is that same book that concludes by describing Moses as one whom God had known "face to face." There are some who claim that the name Israel itself means "those who see God" as well as "those who struggle with God." Surely both of these readings are based in reality.

The warning of Deuteronomy against visual depiction of God must be seen in context. The Bible still saw itself as fighting a surrounding pagan culture in which such depictions were rampant. But even within Israel, the conflict among these Biblical sources may indicate that there was a debate among our most ancient thinkers over the question of God's visibility. This is a debate that accompanies Judaism throughout its history. Philosophers, sages, mystics, and visionaries through the ages have all had their say. In doing so, each of them has added something to the portrait, which still remains unfinished. To be a religious Jew is to walk the tightrope between knowing the invisibility of God and seeing the face of God everywhere. Y-H-W-H is but a breath, utterly without form, the essence of abstraction itself. And yet that same abstraction is the face of God that "peers out from the windows, peeks through the lattice-work." That face contains within it all the faces of humanity, and each of them contains the face of God.

In this sense our religion indeed may be called *incarnational*. The divine presence is incarnate in all the world. God is *ruah kol basar,* the spirit that resides in all flesh. That presence may be brought to consciousness in the mind of every human who is open to it, as it may be blocked out and negated entirely by the closing of the human heart, by cruelty, or by the denial of God's image. The *Shekhinah,* the divine presence in our world, does not dwell where she is not wanted.

MALE AND FEMALE: AN EXCURSUS

Israel sees God in two moments: at the Sea and at Sinai—God the young lover and warrior, God the elderly parent and judge. These are the two primal archetypes of our tradition. Both are powerful and male, but they function psychologically in rather different ways. In the former, Israel is female, epitomized in "the handmaiden at the Sea" who "saw more than Isaiah or Ezekiel." While in the Red Sea context it is the warrior aspect of the young God that is emphasized, this depiction is mostly that of God as lover. This is the religion of Rabbi Akiva, the one who claimed that the Song of Songs, interpreted as referring to the love between God and the Community of Israel, was the "Holy of Holies" of all Holy Scripture. Out of his school there emerged a view that this song was in fact the very essence of all religious teaching and that "had the Torah not been given, the world could have been conducted according to the Song of Songs." Israel, as God's beloved bride, is the one chosen and redeemed by that love. Marriage as a metaphor for the relationship between God and Israel depicts the relationship both as love and as covenant, one in which responsibilities are both mutual and binding. But these flow naturally out of the fullness of love.

In the latter metaphor, Y-H-W-H is the royal father, filled with love for His sometimes wayward son. The tradition is filled with tales of the son exiled from his father's table or the son who has wandered off among the shepherds, forgetting or sometimes even seeking to flee his own royal birth. God as father and king may be an image of power, but as depicted by the rabbis, it is almost always one of love, compassion, and forgiveness. Had Judaism allowed for pictorial representation of God the Father (in the style of Byzantine icons, for example), He would be depicted most commonly with tears in His eyes and open arms, waiting for His children to return to Him.

In later Judaism the balance between these two central metaphors was somehow shifted. God as lover and spouse of Israel was avoided, relegated to esoteric Judaism, the exclusive domain of mystics and poets. The public liturgy as prayed by most Jews was primarily that of father and king. We come before You, says the Rosh Hashanah prayer, "either as children or as servants." But Father/child and King/servant are two faces of the same archetype. The other great image, God as Lover/Spouse/Hero, has been shunted aside. I believe this loss of balance to be one of the tragedies of our *Galut* existence. Some have attributed it to a totemic emasculation, saying that our politically powerless Jewish males could not allow themselves a masculine warrior–lover God, but only an aged father. Others say that Judaism abandoned the younger image because it was too close to "God the Son" of Christianity. Or perhaps this loss was just a part of the general medievalization of Israel's ancient Near Eastern legacy. Whatever the cause, I would suggest that there is reason today to reexamine and revive the language of God as lover and spouse. Both parental and royal metaphors are in deep trouble as pillars of our religious imagination. Kindly and loving as the Jewish father–king God may be, the image still evokes fears of hierarchy and control. This is especially true for

Jewish women seeking a return to their spiritual tradition, who feel themselves excluded from the father–son relationship described here.

The image of God and Israel as a loving pair or as bridegroom and bride brings us face to face with the most intimate side of God. This God is the One who loves us so passionately that the boundaries between us and God disappear in the depths (or heights!) of our love. I referred earlier to the expression that calls the spouse one's "other half." A famous hasidic teacher taught that God and Israel are each "half a form," fulfilled only through longing for and union with each other. The Jewish tradition does not have to insist that this love of God is *agape* rather than *eros;* it understands that generosity of spirit goes hand in hand with the erotic within the bounds of *kiddushin,* the sanctified marital relationship along with the sacred marriage bed.

But the mystical tradition goes farther than seeing God and Israel as lover and beloved. Kabbalah in its fullest development comes to see both partners in this sacred marriage as existing within the divine realm, humanity being either the offspring of this union, or, still more daringly, the wedding attendant who brings the sacred pair together. In this view, *God is both male and female,* a redressing of an imbalance within Jewish monotheism that is especially welcome in our age. It is the union of the feminine *Shekhinah,* or indwelling presence, and the "blessed Holy One," the projected masculine personal God-figure, that is the object of mystical Judaism. To contemporary Jewish mysticism it would be quite clear (as is already hinted at by various earlier kabbalistic sources) that both of these figures exist as a part of the attempt of humanity

to reach forth toward *Eyn Sof,* the limitless and utterly undefined One that alone is ultimately real.

For today's seeker, the image of Israel as God's bride does
not always suffice. However much we seek to liberate this
metaphor from the oppressions of traditional marriage roles,
women have good reason to be suspicious of their depiction
only in the human and never in the divine role. As this
metaphor is transformed by the mystics, male and female are
both liberated from their simple conventional roles. Some
aspects of divinity are male, others female. God is birth-giver,
nursing mother, locked garden, and sea of wisdom, according
to the Kabbalah, as God is wise father, tree of life, and river of
joy. A rich metaphoric imagination, including symbols both
male and female, is part of our legacy. In the past, these
symbols were created and discussed exclusively by men. As
this genre of Jewish creativity becomes open to women's
participation in our day, we will surely see a further rebalancing and greater development of such symbols. All of them
are to be used *le-shem yihud,* to draw us all together back to the
primal One.

The primal pair of male and female is to be identified in one
way or another with that tentative duality we described at the
outset: The God who "fills all the worlds" and the One who
"surrounds all the worlds." Usually, the God within is identified with the female and the God outside with the male,
though these could be reversed as well. The eternal search for
unity that characterizes the Divine is manifest in human life by
the search of men and women for fulfillment in true union
with one another. As we discover the lower unity of God
reflected in all the infinite variety of the universe, so do we

find it in a very particular way in this aspect of the human situation. The God of the Song of Songs, of whom it is said "On my bed at night I sought Him whom my soul loves; I sought Him, but found Him not," is a God fully identified with the human search for fulfillment with the other, a search that is one in all its infinite variety, a search that is real in both its triumphs and its failures.

In the higher unity, of course, these two become one. As the dualities of God and world, of *sovev* and *memale* are meant to be overcome, so too is the duality of male and female. It is a united male–female consciousness that reaches forth to *Eyn Sof*. This union takes place within the individual psyche as well as in the community of men and women. "There is no man without woman, no woman without man, no either of them without *Shekhinah*." This is true within each person as well as of the species as a whole. But it is only by going through the path of this union, rather than seeking to detour around it, that such wholeness can be achieved. Hence Judaism's rejection of celibacy as a religious path.

ONE AND TWO

In the reality of human life unity exists only in fleeting moments. For most of the time we live, and in the regions of our mind that usually occupy us, we remain separate even from those to whom we are most intimately bound. All of us have moments of great union in which we soar toward transcendence. For some, these moments happen in the stillness of nature; for others, they may come with the great interiority of prayer. Some know them best in the course of relationships with those they love. Perhaps a few rare human souls may know all these and more. But every person comes back from such experiences to the world of "self" and "other." That is where we live our lives, do our work, raise our children. The struggle of religious vision is always one of uplifting and transforming the mundane, of making our own separate lives vessels into which the light of unity may flow.

It is for this reason that I continue to use the "God" language of Western theology. In the moments of greatest intimacy within a relationship, we come to realize that separation is but illusory and that oneness represents the greatest truth. The struggle to live in faithfulness to those moments, however, requires the transformation of our ordinary daily lives. This means bringing holiness to bear on the language and experience of *ḥol,* the profane or the merely ordinary. In that consciousness each of us is still a separate being. In order to communicate religious insight to the self that exists at such times, we continue to use the religious language of "self" and "other." The deeper truth remains something of a secret, something with which "the heart seeks to surprise the mind." Hints of the ultimate Oneness of Being have to be found hidden within the dualistic language that the ordinary mind can hear and speak.

The Ba'al Shem Tov was told that redemption would come when "your well-springs spread outward," that is, when others will be able to do as you do, to make real to themselves on a constant basis the existence of the One that underlies the many. His great-grandson, Rabbi Nahman, commented on this that it is only when your teachings reach those "outward" ones, those outside the domain of holiness, that you effect redemption. I would add, and certainly Rabbi Nahman would agree, that "those outside" refers also, or maybe even primarily, to your own self, insofar as you too stand outside *reshut ha-yaḥid,* the domain of the One, and continue to live in the realm of separation. Our religious language has to serve as the vehicle by which our innermost soul can continually educate our ordinary consciousness to its truth.

In the ongoing fascination of our mystics with the name Y-H-W-H, they determined that two of these letters, *Yod* and *Vav,* were "masculine," while the two letters *Heh* were "feminine." This refers both to the shapes of the letters themselves and to various kabbalistic associations that were added to them. In this case, the union of the name, or the proclamation of God's ultimate Oneness, is also the reunion of primal male and primal female. The first letter of the name, *Yod,* is the smallest letter of the alphabet and is described simply as a point. *Yod* is the point of departure, the point from which Divinity first sets out on its great journey into being, the One on the verge of becoming One-in-Many. To speak of God is

to try to speak of the *Yod,* to put into many words that which
is as concentrated and intensely real, yet invisible, as a primal
point, a single point that contains all that will ever be. We too
are at the point of our departure. We have spoken only the first
word, but all else will proceed from this. Torah, our teaching,
is the name of God. We who teach and study it are God's own
face. The rest is commentary.

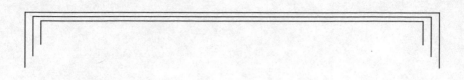

CREATION

One God, Two Ways

One God, but perceived and known in two ways. Y-H-W-H who transcends and surrounds the world and Y-H-W-H who fills the world. The transcendent God is entirely faceless. This God is none other than *Eyn Sof*—that which is without limit, without end, without definition: God as mystery. The God who fills the world has a thousand, a million, a billion, infinite faces. Changing in every moment as the world develops and grows, as generations come and go in the seemingly endless cycle of birth and death, it is both mother and father of these birth cycles, both parent and child. This God is One, known to us in stasis and in movement, in formlessness and in formfulness. The God of stasis is a seated deity, our ancient God depicted as seated on His throne, or the great stone Buddha of Eastern Asia, powerful in their static, eternal, and unchanging character. These seated depictions of the deity are contrasted by dancing gods, shown quite literally that way in the sacred arts of India. Our mystical tradition uses more abstract language, to be sure, but it speaks of God as *sefirot,* ever flowing in and out of one another, as flashing sparks of light, or as *ḥiyyut,* the ever-flowing force of life. All of these may be characterized as "dancing deities," or as dynamic rather than static ways of seeing the Divine. God as the life force, the energy that flows through the body of the universe—that too is certainly a part of our tradition. God is both the source and the flow, the hidden root and the endless branches. We remember always that these two are one. The distinction between "God" and "world" remains a superficial one when Y-H-W-H is one with all of being. "World" is the universe seen in its outward garb; "God" is the same universe when seen from the perspective of its inward core. Bearing this essential point of view in mind, we begin to discuss Creation.

CREATION AND THE JEWISH QUESTION

The fact is that we Jews have largely abandoned Creation as a theological issue. Convinced as we are that the origin of species—and of the universe itself—is something to be explained by scientists rather than theologians, most of us have seen no value in attempting a defense of ancient Jewish views on Creation. If Jews have asked theological questions in this century (one in which theology has surely not been our forté), they are mainly those of revelation ("Did God give the Torah?"), authority ("Then why keep the commandments?"), and providence ("Where was God during the Holocaust?"), but not of Creation. We have left Genesis I in the hands of the so-called Creationists among fundamentalist Christians, circles from which we are quite alienated, both socially and theologically.

But the issue of Creation will not disappear so quickly. The search for meaning and the question of origins do not readily separate from one another. When we ask ourselves what life is all about, why we live and why we die, we cannot help turning to the question of how we got here in the first place. When we try to understand our place in the universe, and especially the relationship of humanity as a whole to the world of nature, we find ourselves returning to the question of Creation. As we seek to extend our notion of community and fellow-feeling to include all *creatures,* seeking out the One within the infinite varieties of the many, we discover that we are still speaking the language of Creation.

We have no essential argument with an evolutionary approach to the tale of life's origins. But we see evolution itself as the greatest of all religious dramas. The history of our universe is the ongoing account of how Y-H-W-H, source of life, reached forth into the world of form, became manifest in the infinite variety of species, and finally became articulate in the consciousness and language of humanity. No blind process is this, but rather the great striving of the One to be manifest in the garb of the many.

More than one voice within contemporary science seems open to describing the origin and evolution of species, in some sense, as the expression of a singular universal force, or as the growth and development of an underlying single organism. While such a force could be conceived as an external Creator, it is more generally seen as a drive within existence that strives relentlessly, though by no means perfectly, toward greater complexity and consciousness. The evolutionary process would then be conceived in a unitive way as the halting, struggling self-assertion of such a singular force or presence, rather than as the endless war of creatures against one another. Such a vision would explain the ongoing emergence of "higher" and more conscious life-forms as evidence of this struggle's emerging success, instead of as the "survival of the fittest."

We recognize that a new Creation story is emerging in our day, one that begins with the origin of matter and reaches onward through the beginnings of plant, animal, and human life. This tale is still unfolding, to be sure, and we nonscientists understand it imperfectly. But we Jews, as bearers of the old Creation tale that for so long nourished and sustained the West's sense of origins and self-understanding, have a special interest in the emerging new story. We are concerned that its ultimate message be one of harmony, one that brings creatures to appreciate their oneness, and does not serve to justify endless conflict. We hope it will retain the strengths of our ancient tale, one that gave each creature its dignity as God's handiwork, gave us humans a special sense of stewardly responsibility, and glorified our rest, our sense of being at peace with all of God's Creation.

We are urgently in need of ways to renew our sense of human responsibility for preserving the natural world around us. As we call for less abusive treatment of earth's resources and a more reverent protection of air, soil, and water, for the preservation of species in both plant and animal realms, we need a theological language that will serve as the basis for such a change in human attitude. The age in which we live cries out for a religious language that speaks of the underlying *unity* of all existence, a unity that is manifest within life's diversity, rather than of the struggle of species against species. This unity is that of Creation, of the sense that all beings emerge from a single source.

We are also tied to Creation and to our ancient tale in the most basic cycle of our religious lives as Jews. I recite the Friday night *kiddush,* which begins with the words "The sixth day; Heaven and earth were completed, they and all their hosts." As the week draws to a close, I know that the creation cycle has happened in my life once again. With the beginning of Shabbat, I bear witness to God's world, whole and created anew. On Friday evening, I testify that I am present to the ongoing work and rest of Y-H-W-H as Creator. This act is an important, even vital one to me. It affirms more than Judaism for me; it affirms my essential humanity, my sense of belonging in this God-filled world, my creation and constant re-creation in God's image.

CREATION AND THE STRUGGLE FOR FAITH

I thus find myself living in an active and symbolically deeply connected way with a story that says God created the world in seven days. I know that I don't believe that story in the literal sense. Neither do I believe in the seven-day Creation, nor am I particularly attracted to the notion that the seven days should be reinterpreted as seven time periods, as seven stages of evolution, or in any other way that seeks to save the literal truth of the text. No, I do not believe it in any ordinary intellectual sense of that term. I also know with all my being that I find this tale both deeply attractive and irresistibly powerful. It draws me to itself, sustains me through the week, and expresses my existence and its meaning. It has become *my own,* so that I choose to live with it in this regular and ever-reaffirming way.

Thus, the simple act of reciting *kiddush* on Friday night leads me to theological crisis. How do I *affirm* that which I do not *believe?* What is the nature of this affirmation in the face of my disbelief? How do we learn to live at peace with these two realities? Rabbi Nahman tells the tale of a prince, well born and noble of character, whose mind was led astray by the intellectual temptations offered him by his royal tutors. Whenever he exercised his mind, he was skeptical of the ancient wisdom on which he had been raised. But when he set that rational mind aside and allowed his heart to speak, he knew that it was true, perhaps true with a depth that he could never articulate in words that would convince his own inquiring mind.

Nahman's prince was still a rare creature in his author's early nineteenth-century universe. But by now, nearly all of us have become that prince. Are we, who refuse to choose between modernity and religious language, condemned to live our lives in constant conflict between heart and mind? Or will we be able to give birth to a new tale of Creation, one that sanctifies our rest and our humanity while also satisfying our search for truth and nourishing our scientific imagination? Can such a new tale, told in other words, come to bear the old tale within it? Or can the old tale be retold in such a way that it contains the new? The real task may be that of integrating our two tales, the one inherited from ages past, and the one emerging from our own spiritual understanding of contemporary science. For a century, these accounts of life's origin have been presented in opposition to one another. The time has come to end that opposition, *to see the two tales as versions of the same story, representing two stages in humanity's own evolving self-understanding.* The time has come when we need to raise our cups over the old tale, aware that it contains the new one being born within it, a drawing together of ancient, contemporary, and timeless truth.

What Comes "First"?

S omewhere within us we intuit that stillness precedes motion. Perhaps this comes as a projection of our own human experience. We imagine silence existing before sound, serving as the *background* from which sound emerges. Darkness seems to us as the condition *prior* to light. There is no inherent reason why any of these should be the case; each of them could as well be reversed. In this same way we see the One as existing *before* the many: unformed being seems simpler than multiplicity. Thus, it intuitively seems *prior* to the countless specific forms that being takes.

This priority is essentially one of primitive logic or of the structure of our thought, rather than one of time. It is in this way that Y-H-W-H of the "upper" unity, the undefined, endless One, precedes Y-H-W-H of the "lower" unity, or God as manifest in the garments of this world. *Sovev,* God in stasis, is still from eternity. מעולם ועד עולם אתה אל—"From world unto world You are God"—alone, unchanging. *Memale,* God in motion, "begins" the dance at some point, sets out on the path that leads through evolution, development, history.

The tale of Creation places this relationship of precedence into a *temporal* framework that is essential to its expression in the language of narrative or myth. Myth is a narrative about that which is beyond narration; in order to bring it into words, it has to be "told" as story. We understand that the story, if it is to work as such, needs *time.* That's the way stories are: some things happen first, other things happen later. There is a temporal order that is essential to the narrative plot. *Once we speak about the relationship of the transcendent unmoved One and the immanent ever-flowing Life Force in narrative terms, we have to invoke time.* Thus we come to Creation. "God created the world" is our Jewish–mythic way of saying "The One precedes—and enters into—the many."

This view essentially sees Creation as emanation: the "act" about which we speak is really a process, a flowing forth of the divine self, rather than the creation of a wholly other out of nothing. It is divinity *becoming* universe, or pure being garbing itself in forms, rather than a specific deity *creating* a universe outside itself. We also understand that this emanation process is a timeless one: to speak of Y-H-W-H before emanation is to construct a reality truly beyond our understanding. Our religious *language* continues to be that of Creation, just as our liturgy continues to speak of God in personal metaphors. But its meaning has shifted in this significant way.

From the time our sages encountered the philosophy of Greece, they insisted that God had created the world *Yesh me-ayin,* "being out of nothingness." Against Aristotle's view that matter could be neither created nor destroyed, and was therefore eternal, Jewish thinkers held fast to that which they considered the biblical faith. They did so even though the Bible had no clear position on the nature of Creation, except that it was a freely willed act of Y-H-W-H, effected by the power of divine speech. Many interpreters of the Torah had long claimed that the *tohu va-bohu* ("formlessness and void") of Genesis 1:2 in fact referred to some "prime matter" or earlier state of being, out of which Creation took place. The early rabbis seem to have had such views; they spoke of "the treasuries of snow beneath God's Throne of Glory" as the

stuff of which the world had been formed. But all these views
were set aside, or even condemned as folly, in the drive to
purify our view of Creation, to say that Y-H-W-H did it all
alone, with no prior existence to help Him, and out of pure
nothingness. Such was the philosophers' selective reading of
the older rabbinic sources. But then the mystics of Judaism
undertook a truly remarkable reversal of language and meaning. The *ayin* (or "nothingness") out of which being emerged,
they claimed, was in fact *God's own deepest self.* God's act of
Creation begins with a turning inward. It is within the divine
nihil, the nothingness that is God, that Creation takes place.
The divine nothing (perhaps better "No-thing"), so called
because it had been utterly empty, without form, beyond
reach, beyond description, in the moment of Creation reveals
itself also to be the "All-thing," the source from which all
being emerges and the flowing fount by which all is sustained.

Two Tales

The traditions of Israel offer us two tales of Creation that may come to be placed on a more equal footing in the Judaism we pass on to future generations. First is the biblical tale in Genesis 1, in which God *speaks* the world into being. The universe is divine articulation, the unspoken inner self of divinity put into reality by means of language or the creative word. The oneness of silence becomes the multiplicity of words or things, both referred to as *devarim* in Hebrew. This multiplicity begins with the first *yehi*, "let there be," a word closely related to the name of God. From there it becomes all words, all language, all the variety of life, seen as the unending verbalization of the great divine silence. Once the well of that silence is plumbed, the gush of *devarim*, of constant creation through language, never ceases. Were the flow of divine speech to be halted even for an instant, some hold, the entire cosmos would return to nothingness. The power of this account in the formation of the Jewish psyche is well known. We are a civilization of language, one that bears endless respect and affection for the written or spoken word.

Side by side with this ancient tale, the kabbalists offer another. According to this account, the world is *born*, rather than spoken, out of God. Here we are called to take note of the first letter *Heh* of the divine name. This letter is associated with the inner divine womb and the act of birth. This face of God is that of primal mother, the divine as life giver, as nourishing and sustaining source. It is from this God-womb that all variety is born. The primal point of *Yod* has here revealed itself to be an ever-giving font of life in *Heh*. This *Heh* is the womb of oneness out of which all the multiple varied offspring will be born. Variety emerges first in the multiple faces of God, but flows onward to include all faces and all bodies of the universe. Each of us comes out of this single source in the One, and all of us ever turn back to it. *Teshuvah,* or return to Y-H-W-H, as we shall see later, is also an eternal movement, an ongoing return to the womb of God. Contemplation, says the father of all kabbalists, is an act of nursing at the divine breast.

Whichever of these two accounts we use, we want to be careful to articulate it in a way that keeps faith with our vision of oneness: the word as spoken is never fully separate from its speaker; the child remains deeply connected to and nourished by the one who gives it birth. Here, perhaps unlike the human analogy, separation is only superficial. We think that we are separate in order to function as separate minds and beings. But, in a deeper sense, we know that there has been no separation at all. We remain a part of that divine source that spoke us into being or gave us birth.

THE ONE AND THE MANY

In this theological context, to ask the question "Why did God create the world?" is to ask too fully within the framework of the myth. In Yiddish, this is called *a kashe oif a mayse,* "an objection to a story." Stories should be allowed to stand on their own merit as stories, free from intellectualized objections. The question assumes not only the temporal precedence of God to world but also a will of God in an overly anthropomorphic sense. The question should better be put, in our context: "Why is reality the way it is? Why does human consciousness experience itself as separate, but bear within it intimations of a greater oneness? *If all is one, on some deeper or truer level of existence, why do we experience life as so fragmented? Why are there many faces, rather than just the one?*"

In seeking to answer these questions, we have to enter into the dialectics of what Jewish writers call *tsimtsum* and *hitpashtut,* or divine contraction and divine flow. In discussing Creation while holding fast to oneness, we cannot help but speak the language of paradox. Creation may be depicted as the first act of divine self-revelation, Y-H-W-H coming out of hiding, the One revealing itself in the garb of nature. But this revelation takes place through an act of hiding, for the One is now cloaked within the many. This two-sided process, a self-revelation of God that comes about through the hiding or cloaking of the divine Self, begins in the first moment of Creation, and repeats itself constantly in each moment that Creation is renewed.

The God of stillness begins to enter into the dance of motion. The undefined One puts on the coat of many colors. In this, the One is seeking, as it were, to enter into a world of infinite variety so that its oneness might be attested to the ultimate degree. *Only in that garbing does the Divine sufficiently hide itself that it might be revealed.*

Within being, there is an endless drive for manifestation in ever new and varied forms, a drive we see manifest as a life force, but that exists beyond the bounds of what we call "animate" as well. As that force drives ever forward for growth and change, the oneness that it bears within it is stretched ever further. Thus is the One renewed in its singularity, as each new form turns out to be naught but itself once again. The One renews itself by stretching forth into the realm of the many. This drive toward self-extension, ever testing the limits of selfhood, as it were, is the One's search for its "other." The inherent tendency toward variety and diversity, combined with the constant reaching toward more complex forms of life, culminates, according to our ancient tale, in the creation of humanity, the crowning achievement of the "sixth day." Only when a self-conscious human being has emerged, one who can both acknowledge the One and insist on the separateness of individual identity, has the test of self-extension begun to reach its goal. We humans are thus the divine helpmate; the *ezer ke-negdo,* both the partner and the one who stands "over against," or "as opposed to." In the very "otherness" of our self-conscious minds, we serve to confirm the existence of the One.

The fact that procreation throughout the higher forms of life, animal as well as human, requires the partnership of male and female, is nature's representation of this essential quality

of searching for the other, of longing for fulfillment in union–
reunion, which lies at the very base of all existence. In seeing
ourselves as living in need of partnership with another for true
fulfillment (a man without a wife is called "half a body" by the
Zohar), we represent, in human form, the search of the eternal
One. This is yet another way in which we are "God's image,"
though here the likeness is shared with other living creatures
as well.

To say it differently, the testimony that God is One requires
the presence of an other. Who else can bear witness to that
Oneness? But God has no other, no one to whom to be
revealed, no one to say "There you are!" The divine One seeks
out an other for reasons that we do not fully understand; the
One that is beyond division becomes divided and enters into
this universe of fragmentation so that there is one who can
respond to it, one who can affirm its reality, one who can both
know it as real and love it as "other." Self-revelation requires
encounter between self and other; the revealer needs an other
to whom to be revealed. The flow of divine energy, which we
experience as God's love for the world, needs to step outside
itself. Love needs another. There must be someone to witness,
to appreciate, even to respond. Hide-and-seek just doesn't
work as solitaire! But how can there be such an other if life is
naught but an infinite coloring of varied manifestations of the
One? The God who is all can have no other. Here the divine
light has to hide itself that it might be revealed. It withdraws
itself from being in order that it might be seen, in order to
allow for us to exist as "other," so that we might see and bear
witness to it. This paradox of divine self-withdrawal is what
the Jewish sages call *tsimtsum*.

The intensity of divine light is so great that it allows for the

existence of no other. Were this light to be revealed fully, all
sense of separate identity would pass away, and "we" would
be naught but part of the endless One. But the "other" is the
very purpose of that flow of life in the first place. The im-
mortal and eternal seeks to be known by its opposite, the
mortal and temporal. But what room is there for the mortal
and temporal to exist if all is the flow of divinity? Therefore,
divine light has to be withheld, and we are given the gift
(however illusory) of existence as separate beings, individual
mortals, who struggle and rejoice our way through a transitory life. In order to be God's "other," we have to be all that
the eternal One is not: transitory, corporeal, mortal. God, as it
were, seeks out an opposite—and a partner—in us.

WHO IS AT THE CENTER?

B ut do we really want to say that "God creates the universe *in order* to create the human being?" In our tradition, the debate between advocates of the theocentric and the anthropocentric universe has existed for a long time. Maimonides, in view of the evidence of science and philosophy in his time, rejected the anthropocentric worldview of the early rabbis, one that claimed clearly that God had created the world for the sake of humans, and indeed for the sake of Israel, or "the righteous." The kabbalists responded to Maimonides by reasserting the anthropocentric point of view in new terms. Maimonides' universe was one that left no room, they felt, for the significance of human action. What difference could it make to the abstract Maimonidean God whether we existed or not, whether we fulfilled the *mitsvot* or not? They created an image of the universe in which God is incomplete without human action, in which the role of humanity in the process of *tikkun* (cosmic restoration), or the establishment of divine sovereignty, is a crucial one.

Recent discussions of this subject, largely in the environmentalist community, have tried to speak for a *biocentric* rather than either a theocentric or an anthropocentric worldview. Both of these views, it is claimed, for different reasons, have led to human neglect of responsible action with regard to protecting and preserving life as a whole. The anthropocentric view has tended toward human arrogance, a view that only human life and human creations are worthy of serious attention, whereas the theocentric view is antiworldly altogether, not seeing in material existence itself a fit object for true or urgent concern. Both of these critiques are somewhat simplistic, using as "straw men" highly reductionist versions of these religious outlooks. The fact is that theocentrism, at least as represented in Judaism, has also led to a strong sense of religious obligation to act, a heteronomous ethic in which we are commanded by the One "above" to act in a responsible manner. It is the anthropocentric view, seeing humans as the "crown" of creation, that gives birth to the notion of stewardship and guardianship over the divine creation. Both of these are potentially valuable allies in the fashioning of a more responsible human viewpoint. *Rather than fight or denounce these parts of our human legacy, our job is to see that they are used in ways that increase, rather than diminish, our sense of collective responsibility.*

In a nondualistic worldview, the sharp edges are taken off this debate. If the One is the center of the cosmos, that hardly means that the human or the natural is at the periphery of significance. Still, we must somehow take our place in this ancient conversation. The question is given new focus in our time because the magnitude of the universe has made us so much smaller. We speak of a world that is not 6,000 years old, but whose age reaches into billions of years. We speak of a universe not of one planet with a *raki'a*—firmament—above it, and God sitting on a throne just beyond it, but of one with infinite numbers of stars in infinite numbers of galaxies, set in a space so vast it can hardly be measured or imagined. How hard it is to say, in such a world, that the purpose of it all was this speck of earth and this brief moment of transitory human life!

Here too, we may be guided by an alternative voice from

within our own tradition. The tale of Creation, as told in Genesis, indeed seems to view human beings as the final goal, created in the moment just before God enters into rest and celebrates the world's completion. Later versions of that story make the point even more explicit. Adam and Eve are like the guests at a banquet; everything is prepared for them before they arrive. But other parts of the Bible itself seem to take issue with this view of humanity's place in the universe. The Psalmist sees a great chorus of beings singing hallelujahs to their God. Humans are just part of this symphony of praise, one where "elders and youths, young men and maidens" take their place together with "mountains and hills, fruit-trees and cedars; wild beasts and cattle, creeping things and winged birds." Another Psalm describes the great panorama of Creation as beginning when God spread forth the heavens like a garment of light. In this luminous cosmos, each creature is given its particular place, human alongside stork, mountain-goat, hare, and young lion. Of all of them together, the author exclaims, "How manifold are your works, O Y-H-W-H, You have made them all in wisdom."

Nowhere is this view more fully expressed than in the closing chapters of the Book of Job, the great biblical testimony to the struggle with life's meaning and divine justice. Job's challenge to God is finally answered, and God's speeches there are truly among the most elevated religious documents of all time. But the answer given to Job is not one that defends God as a just actor on the stage of human history. Job is given no reason for his suffering, no explanation of his children's deaths, or his own affliction. Rather, he is shown the magnificence of God's universe, the great and wondrous creatures that extend far beyond human reach or human understanding.

He is shown that the human world is but an infinitesimal part of this universe, one far too vast and too magnificent to be embraced by the mind of mortals. It is in seeing these, and realizing both his own smallness and his own place within a vast and glorious cosmos, that God's challenger finds his consolation.

EVOLUTION: AN ONGOING PROCESS

T hen what shall we say of our place in the universe? It seems fair to say no more than this: the One strives to evolve itself into ever more complex, advanced, and conscious forms of existence, whether these exist only here, or in another manner in other worlds as well. Our religious understanding of evolution means that the divine energy is ever reaching forward and upward, in whatever halting and often multiple and spiralling (and not always successful!) ways, toward more sophisticated and complex levels of development. *From where we stand in the evolutionary process,* and given our ignorance of extraterrestrial conscious life-forms, it seems right to say that human consciousness is a significant and qualitative leap in this process. There may be other such leaps that we neither see nor understand. But insofar as we understand things, it is we humans alone on this planet who are able to conceive, and thus respond *consciously,* to the inner force that pulses through us and all being. Of course, all of life is a response of sorts to that force, but even the poetic vision to depict it that way is itself a human creation. Consciousness is a unique form of response to the One. Our response may be entirely primitive. It is perfectly conceivable that we are at the very *earliest* stages of evolution when it comes to consciousness of the One and openness to higher states of conscious life. The future evolution of human (or even "posthuman") mind and consciousness may well reach far beyond our grasp.

It is only from where we stand in the process that the human is seen as the apex of existence. Even this is true only insofar as we stretch our minds and souls to serve as the conscious and self-aware articulation of a universal force that goes far beyond us. Our position in the theocentric–anthropocentric debate is thus a dialectical or paradoxical one: *Ḥaviv Adam she-nivra batselem:* the human is beloved only because we are the mirror-reflection, the portrait, of the divine self. Our human greatness is best shown when we understand ourselves as part of, rather than as over against, the universe of God's Creation.

Humanity is defined and distinguished from other forms of life in our tradition by the term *medabber;* the human is a "speaker." It is speech, we are told, that separates us from the animal kingdom. Speech and thought develop hand in hand. I would say that we *are* an articulation of the divine self that was inconceivable before our human existence. It is only persons who can understand themselves as going forth on the journey to bring back portraits of the King. That is the task of consciousness alone. We are life articulate, being that has become self-conscious. But the voice we bear within us is that of Y-H-W-H. The psalm of all existence is sung within each creature and all around us. We humans only write the lyrics.

The evolutionary process surely does not end with the advent of humans. Within the history of humanity we continue to see this process ever at work. Nowhere is this more manifest than in the growth of our images, ideas, and understandings of God. This too is part of the evolutionary process, *the divine growing within the human mind,* seeking to be known in ever more refined and subtle ways. Human mind and imagination continually strive to comprehend and give expression to the cosmos in which we live. This is true in terms of both mind and soul. Human mind gives expression to the divine as intellect, striving ever toward greater abstraction and immateriality. The human heart gives expression to that same divinity in the form of devotion, including the need to put forth those names and faces of the One that so aid us in our worship. It is no accident that biblical thought combined the function of mind and soul in the notion of *lev,* or heart. We continue to insist that they be seen as one.

Insofar as we can see things, then, we human beings may be the cutting edge of cosmic evolution. We recognize that such an assertion is also the cutting edge of *hybris,* and that it must always be used only to humble us with the mantle of service and to join us to others, not to set us up as above the rest of Creation. That would indeed be idolatry in the tradition of Pharaoh, who worshipped himself as a god.

By a stretching of our mind and our soul, we come to know and love the One. It is only the need for this stretching that allows us both to be ourselves and to fulfill our role in awareness of Y-H-W-H. We walk "on a path between fields of fire and fields of ice," according to the ancient rabbis. Our position with regard to knowing God is rather like that of life's dependence on earth's distance from the sun. Were we any closer, were divinity any more readily to be found in this world, we would be "burned" in the fields of fire, reabsorbed into the oneness of the All by the readiness of divine touch. Were we any farther, were the presence of the divine reality any less accessible than it is, we would be "frozen" by our distance from the One, unable to find the truth. We exist in such a way that only by a constant striving to achieve openness of mind and soul can we approach our goal. It is the openness of these two faculties, intellect and emotion, that combines to create the religious life.

But Creation is only the first stage, the first mode of relationship between the human and the divine. We recognize the One in Creation, the presence of Y-H-W-H in all of being. As that presence calls out to us, makes demands on us, and causes us to reshape our lives, the modalities of revelation and redemption will be joined to that of Creation. Here it will become clear to us that mind and heart do not in themselves suffice, but that *action* must be joined to them as their third partner, indeed as the central area of their fulfillment, if the religious life is to fulfill its purpose.

FROM *AGGADAH* TO *HALAKHAH*

Thus far, our discussion has remained in the realm of *aggadah* (literally, "narrative"), the literary, theological, and philosophical portion of the Jewish heritage. Traditional Jewish teaching is divided into *aggadah* and *halakhah* (literally, "the path"), or the normative and binding aspect. Judaism in our day is deeply impoverished in *both* of these areas. Most Jews, with the exception of an Orthodox minority, have opted out of the authority system of classical *halakhah*. I believe that a new, though much less rigid, *halakhah* will emerge for Jews in the new era of Jewish history that is just beginning, a *halakhah* that we are not yet ready to define. But a new *halakhah* will only proceed from a new *aggadah:* halakhic practice is the crystallization into form of a nexus of ideas, beliefs, hopes, and legends. It is these we must first seek to reinterpret and even to recreate for our age. *Aggadah,* too, has become diminished in our times. Jews have lost the art of thinking richly around the narratives and events that make up the core of our faith. I have thus begun this discussion of Creation from an aggadic viewpoint. We now, however, must turn from *aggadah* to *halakhah*. No Jewish theology can avoid the questions of demand and responsibility. These are essential elements of the legacy of both prophets and sages. A particular statement of faith is only meaningful in a Jewish context when it becomes the source of *mitsvah*. Until we ask ourselves "What does this position *demand* of me?" or "What *obligations* will I take on in my life to make this position a reality?" we have not yet asked the serious Jewish questions.

In the past Judaism has tended to root all of *halakhah* in the single event of the revelation at Mount Sinai, leaving the other critical events of our faith-narrative mostly bereft of halakhic component. Perhaps it is time for a change and a rebalancing of this division. I would suggest that *each* of our many tales contains within it elements of both *halakhah* and *aggadah.* As we retell these tales, we must ask ourselves questions of obligation and commitment. What action directives will derive from my statement of commitment to this ancient story and from my particular rereading of it? How is my life changed by the fact that I see myself descended from those who came forth from Egypt? As an heir to those who built the Temple and those who saw it destroyed? What does it mean to the way I live that I bear within me the tale of Cain and Abel? Of Abraham and Isaac? Of Naomi and Ruth?

With regard to Creation, there are *mitsvot* on several levels that derive from our commitment to the retelling of the tale. Faith in Creation makes demands in the areas of both those *mitsvot* that lead to the personal fulfillment of divinity in our lives, and those that lead to the greater realization of the divine presence in the universe as a whole. All *mitsvot* exist for the same purpose: the increased realization of divinity in the world through the agency of those who perform the *mitsvah.* Hasidic authors liked to associate the word *mitsvah* with the Aramaic *tsavta,* meaning "togetherness." A *mitsvah* is an act in which person and God are joined together. Some *mitsvot* bring about realization of divinity largely through the greater awareness or higher level of devotion in which those persons performing the mitsvah, and they alone, are engaged. Other *mitsvot* are acts of "sanctifying the divine name" because they are shared with an entire community. We Jews have always placed a higher value on these for their public character. Still others bring about greater presence of divinity in the world, because they enhance the lives of needy humans and lessen their suffering. Some of the *mitsvot* called for by Creation are personal, others communal, and still others enhance divinity because they contribute to the prolonged and bettered existence of the natural world itself.

The First *Mitsvah:* Be Aware

The first *mitsvah* that proceeds from our faith in Creation is that of awareness itself. As a Scriptural basis for it, we can surely turn to Deuteronomy 4:39: "Know this day and set it upon your heart that Y-H-W-H is God in heaven above and on the earth beneath; there is none else." The One above or beyond the world and the One within the world are the same—that is the ultimate knowledge to be absorbed by both mind and heart. The obligation to become and to remain aware of divine presence is the foundation of all religious life. It is achieved by a combination of spontaneity and discipline. While the spontaneous aspect of awareness, an opening of eyes, by definition cannot be encased in form, the regular discipline of awareness can; this is the "setting upon your heart."

Surely one of the great gifts of Creation is found in the two daily periods of the change of light, the hours of dawn and sunset. "Know this day" suggests that we may learn from the nature of the day itself. There is a quality of being in those moments when light changes, as day begins and day ends, that naturally leads to a deep inner silence. It is the great wisdom of our tradition to have proclaimed these hours as the two daily prayer times, and their celebration as such ideally remains central to the religious life of the Jew. *Being awake and aware as sun rises and sun sets can make a difference in our religious lives that cannot be overestimated.* The Ba'al Shem Tov, one of the great Jewish prayer masters of all time, is said to have warned his disciples about the danger, and indeed near-vanity, of reciting morning prayers after the sun was already up.

In God's Image

The second *mitsvah* of Creation is that of treating every human being as the image of God. The very core of our self-understanding as Jews and as persons calls upon us to see each man and woman as a lens through which the Divine is reflected. This simple statement is the basis for all Jewish interpersonal ethics. When Rabbi Akiva claimed that "Love your neighbor as yourself; I am the Lord" (Leviticus 19:18) was the basis of the entire Torah, his colleague Ben Azai replied that "This is the book of the generations of Adam; on the day when God made humans they were fashioned in the image of God" (Genesis 5:1) was a more basic principle than that. The discussion is a crucial one for understanding the place of ethical conduct within Judaism. Akiva is the great believer in love, both human and divine. Akiva sees the Song of Songs as the central metaphor for the relationship between God and Israel; he is willing to allow human ethics to base themselves on the commandment to love. Ben Azai is more realistic. Even where there is no love, he tells us, there is still the divine image. Every person is the bearer of that image and is entitled to the esteem and reverence in which we hold the face of God.

All the decisions we make in the interpersonal realm need to bear this principle in mind. The decision to open ourselves to another in love is one of sharing that divine spark within us, that of seeking out the face of God within the other. The realization that every human being is God's image makes an unambiguous demand upon us. Each person has the right to be known and loved for that divine image that is his or her most profound and often hidden self. Each image of God in the world also has the right to exist in dignity, to engage in meaningful labor, and to live at peace. The role of governments and political parties is to see that this happens; it is to this standard of our religious respect for human dignity that they are to be held up. In our individual lives as well, we constantly face the question, "Am I treating human beings— myself as well as others—as the image of God?" This demand will shape and restrict our actions rather clearly in attempts at the "use" of other human beings—whether as sexual objects, as tools to help us gain money on political power, or as fulfillment of some other need we have. We even ignore the divine image when we place people in depersonalized categories, relating to them only professionally, as "clients" of our therapeutic practice, or as "congregants" of our synagogue.

When applied to the way we treat *ourselves,* it will restrict both those activities that harm the human body, and those that lead us into situations of personal degradation. It is the basis of that hard-to-define term *menschlichkeyt,* or decent humanity, that sets the agenda for the instinctive ethics of many Jews, even those cut off from the theological moorings of their own values. The value of *tselem Elohim,* seeing humans as God's image, is also key to some of the most wrenching and difficult decisions we face in our lives. Some of these decisions, such as those involving abortion and euthanasia, are still difficult and morally ambiguous, even where we do seek full regard for God's image. Consideration of the human as divine image does not necessarily tell us which way to turn in such situations. Even there, however, it is a principle that guides us away from steps that might otherwise be undertaken too lightly.

But the matter of treating each person as the image of God extends beyond all these examples of moral demand. If we really live as though each person were God's image, we necessarily find every human being to be *of interest* to us. "There is no person who does not have his hour"—every human life has something unique and valuable about it, a contribution to be offered that can be fulfilled by no other. Each messenger brings back a *unique* portrait of the king, one that only he or she could paint. To take seriously our faith that each person is God's image is to treat every person with a spiritual dignity and caring that would transform all of our lives. Surely none of us lives this *mitsvah* to the fullest, but there can be no Judaism that does not constantly attempt to make it a reality.

CELEBRATING CREATION:
THE *MITSVAH* OF *SHABBAT*

A third *mitsvah* that Creation calls upon us to fulfill is that of the Sabbath. The Sabbath is surely the greatest gift that the people Israel has to offer to civilization in terms of the forms of religious life. *Shabbat* is an extended meditation on the wonders of the created world and the divine presence that fills it. The weekly stopping of the clock and relief from all pressures and obligations of the workday world, from the ongoing demand to recreate and transform reality, is needed more than ever in our fast-paced world. It gives us the opportunity to enjoy the world as we have received it and to bask in its holy light. *Shabbat* is, if you will, *contemplation turned into a way of living.* Rather than the lone and silent contemplative act, which lies at the heart of all prayer, *Shabbat* is that same contemplation turned into the mode of family and communal joy and celebration. In its ideal form, it is an exquisite sharing with those we love of our awareness that we, the world around us, and that love itself, are all gifts from the one source of life.

This is not the place to elaborate on precisely how the Sabbath should be celebrated. Ultimately, it should be a day of joy and not restriction. The rules for *Shabbat* exist in order to create the sacred time in which the transformation of consciousness that is *Shabbat's* real meaning may take place. This observer has found that many of the larger rules make sense. Avoidance of travel, of commerce, and of all forms of schedule watching and weekday obligation seem to lie at the core of the *Shabbat* experience. The finer details of *Shabbat* observance will have to be tried and tested by each seeker or community. Some will do better with more of the traditional *halakhah,* others with less, depending largely on individual needs for structure or freedom. But some sort of halakhic form should be firmly established, for it is this that creates the needed "fence" within which *Shabbat* consciousness can live.

"To Work It and Guard It": Preserving God's World

A fourth and very different *mitsvah* area that proceeds directly from this religion of Creation is that of acting with concern for the healthy survival of Creation itself. As we seek to articulate a Judaism appropriate to a new era of Jewish history, we cannot fail to note that this period begins in the same decades when the human race realizes it has achieved the gruesome possibility of destroying the planet on which we all live. The rabbis tell us that shortly after Adam was created, God walked him around the Garden of Eden and told him to take care to guard the world that he was being given. "If you destroy this world," he was told, "there is no one to come and set it right after you." Such an *aggadah* has a level of intense meaning in our age that the early rabbis could hardly have foretold.

Telling the tale of Creation is itself a statement of love of the natural world. It needs to be accompanied by actions that bear witness to that love—without these it is false testimony. The ethic that proceeds from this tale is one of strong commitment to *ahavat ha-bri'ot,* the love of all God's creatures, and a sense of absolute responsibility for their survival. (For us Jews, after all, love and responsibility always go hand in hand!) This is a worldview in which the love of God and love for the world, including both the natural and the human dimensions, are in no way separable from one another. A piety that proclaims the love of God, without showing it by a love for world, is theologically self-contradictory. It is the natural world that embodies the only God we know. The tale of Creation achieves its fulfillment in acts we undertake to make our appreciation of divinity real by the way we live. We do so both in our individual personal lives and in the commitments we make to greater causes. The needs of the world are so great and so urgent that they cannot be adequately addressed only by a life of personal purification that creates a "holy" elite, but does nothing more to help the world survive.

Here, too, the details are hard to specify, and each person and community has to find ways to fulfill these commandments. By way of example, it surely seems right that we achieve a high level of consciousness and action regarding the ways we live, the products we use, and the ways we dispose of them. We must stop being callous and excessive users of earth's resources. We must become aware and share with others the realization that a small minority of the human race consumes far more than its appropriate share of earth's resources. We need to concern ourselves with the continued availability for generations to come of pure air, pure water, and good earth that will yield untainted produce. As good Jewish parents, concerned always with providing for our children, we must not allow ourselves to consume the legacy that belongs to future generations. The many areas in which to become active in ways helpful to the world's survival hardly need enumerating here. Each of us must find significant means to become partners in giving attention to such concerns. The fact that we band together in such activities with persons of good will who relate to the divine through other traditions (or without the language of traditional religion), is all for the good. There is an authentic *kiddush ha-Shem* in expressions of our Jewish faith that can be shared in such a way with others. The example of Abraham and Sarah, who fulfilled their love of God by making God beloved to others, is the starting point of our renewal of the Jewish moral life. The open tent of our first parents, into which all were welcomed and where all were fed and taught by example, must once again be open to others in our old–new home.

Another series of *mitsvot* that proceeds directly from a relationship with this Creation tale is that which is called in Hebrew by the general term *tsa'ar ba'aley ḥayyim* ("the suffering of living beings"), or sympathy with pain caused to animals. Our story of Creation tells us that we humans were created on the same day as were the land animals. Here again, even within the Genesis tale, we are being told that we are less separable from the animal kingdom than other aspects of that story may lead us to think. The Creation tale also makes us rulers over the animal kingdom, but only as God's viceroy who bears responsibility to the ultimate Ruler. This role demands of us that we be sympathetic to the suffering of other creatures, and that we not cause them needless pain. A commitment to preserving the earth also means a commitment to preserving the great and wondrous variety of life species in which the One is manifest.

VEGETARIANISM:
A *KASHRUT* FOR OUR AGE

In this spirit, I believe the time has come for us to reconsider the question of whether we should continue to consume animal flesh as food. Our tradition has always contained within it a certain provegetarian bias, even though it has provided for the eating of meat. In the ideal state of Eden, according to the Bible, humans ate only plants; we and the animals together were given the plants as food. Only after the expulsion from Eden, when the urge overwhelmed humans and led them toward evil, did the consumption of flesh begin. The very first set of laws given to humanity sought to limit this evil by forbidding the flesh of a still-living creature, placing a limit on acts of cruelty or terror related to the eating of animal flesh. The Torah's original insistence that domestic animals could be slaughtered only for purpose of sacrifice, an offering to God needed to atone for the killing, was compromised only when the Book of Deuteronomy wanted to insist that sacrifice be offered in Jerusalem alone. Realizing that people living at a great distance could not bring all their animals to the Temple for slaughter, the "secular" slaughter and eating of domestic animals was permitted. Even then, the taboo against consuming blood, and later, the requirement to salt meat until even traces of blood were removed, "for the blood is the self" of the creature, represent a clear discomfort with the eating of animal flesh. Most significantly, the forbidding of any mixing of milk and meat represents a proto-vegetarian sensibility. Milk is the fluid by which life is passed on from generation to generation; it may not be consumed with flesh, representing the taking of that life in an act of violence. The fluid of life may not be mixed with that of death. As the Torah says of the hewn-stone altar: "For you have waved your sword over it and have profaned it."

The reasons for acting upon this vegetarian impulse in our day are multiple and compelling, *just as compelling, I believe, as the reasons for the selective taboos against certain animals must have been when the Community of Israel came to accept these as the word of God.* This is what we mean, after all, when we talk about a *mitsvah* being "the word of God" or "God's will." It is a form of human expression or a way of acting that feels compellingly right. This rightness has both a moral and a spiritual dimension; it is an expression of values we choose, but it also makes a more profound statement about who we are. We then come to associate it with divinity, and it becomes a vehicle through which we express our spiritual selves. With the passage of time, origins are shrouded in mystery, and the form becomes the "will of God." Israelites of ancient times felt that way about the taboos widely current in their society against the consumption of certain animals that they saw as repulsive, against the eating of blood, the mixing of milk and meat, and so forth. They associated this series of taboos with the God of Sinai. Over the centuries, *kashrut* as we know it became a *mitsvah*, a way in which Jews are joined to God.

Our situation has certain important parallels to this one. We are urgently concerned with finding a better way to share earth's limited resources. We know that many more human lives can be sustained if land is used for planting rather than for grazing of animals for food. We are committed also to a healthier way of living and are coming to recognize that the human is, after all, a mostly vegetarian species. But for us as Jews, the impulse is largely a moral and religious one. We have a long tradition of abhorring violence. Cruelty to animals has long been forbidden by Jewish law and sensibilities. Our tradition tells us that we must shoo a mother bird away from the nest before we take her eggs so that she does not suffer as we break the bond between them. We are told that a mother and her calf may not be slaughtered on the same day. The very next step beyond these prohibitions is a commitment to a vegetarian way of living.

We Jews in this century have been victims of destruction and mass slaughter on an unprecedented scale. We have seen every norm of humanity violated as we were treated like cattle rather than human beings. Our response to this memory is surely a complex and multitextured one. But as we overcome the understandable first reactions to the events, some of us feel our abhorrence of violence and bloodshed growing so strong that it reaches even beyond the borders of the human and into the animal kingdom. We Jews, who always looked upon killing for sport or pleasure as something alien and repulsive, should now, out of our own experience, be reaching the point where we find even the slaughter of animals for food morally beyond the range of the acceptable. If Jews have to be associated with killing at all in our time, let it be only for the defense of human life. Life has become too precious in this era for us to be involved in the shedding of blood, even that of animals, when we can survive without it. This is not an ascetic choice, we should note, but rather a life-affirming one. A vegetarian Judaism would be more whole in its ability to embrace the presence of God in all of Creation.

Human Love and Human Pain

Our willingness to see God within the natural and human orders can be a source of pain as well as pleasure in our lives. Ours has always been a strongly nonmonastic tradition. We view human love and true attachment to others in an entirely positive light. Our ability to love and to live in familial relationships and in close friendship are testimony to the image of God in which we are made. But that very ability to love is also a great source of human suffering. The very natural human drive to form attachments with others leads us to feel so keenly the pain we know when those we love are hurt or are taken from us. Caring and hurting go together in the human experience. There is no allowing ourselves to love that does not entail our making ourselves vulnerable. This vulnerability inevitably makes for pain. It is the very best in us, our ability to open ourselves and to discover the divine image in the other, that also allows us to be so terribly hurt. This is the way the human being is designed. Sometimes we feel it is a flaw in our making. Yet we know we would not want to hand over the ability to love for protection against pain and loss. The human situation may indeed be a cruel one, but we are not in a position to change it essentially, only to make it more bearable through a measure of understanding.

This applies as well to the pain faced by individuals that is not due to relations with others. Our vulnerability to illness, accident, and other forms of tragic hurt, are essential parts of our mortality. While we could imagine a neater and cleaner world, one in which all human beings might live to a predetermined age and then die without pain or anxiety, to make room for the next generation, such is not human life as we know it. The insecurity of existence and our lack of knowledge about what each tomorrow will bring are part of what gives us the frailty that makes us human.

It is in a nontraditional and yet somehow more than a metaphorical sense that we say God cares about and participates in human pain. If the human mind is part of that great collective mind that makes up God, and if the human heart is part of the one great heart that is God's, then human suffering is a part of the legacy that remains forever bound up in the divine One. Such bits of human reality, including both love and pain, which indeed seem utterly minuscule in the whole divine scheme of things, nevertheless have their place within the ongoing reality of Y-H-W-H and do not belong to us as individuals alone.

The rabbis say that whoever takes a human life negates the divine image in the world. We might extend this to say that whoever causes suffering to a human being brings pain to the presence of God as it is manifest in that person. In this sense, we say that a *Shekhinah* who loves and cares is also a *Shekhinah* who hurts, who suffers with us in our pain and loss. Among the hasidic teachings that have moved me most deeply is an interpretation of the verse "You shall be holy, for I the Lord your God am holy" as a petition, rather than as a command. "Wherever you go I am there within you," says the *Shekhinah* to the person. "Therefore, please don't take me any place defiled." The divine within the person is hurt by defilement and asks to be shielded from this needless pain. I would say the same about suffering itself: the pain inflicted upon a person is inflicted upon the divine presence that dwells within that person as well. A way of life that avoids doing harm to human beings (including oneself), as well as to animals, is a way of life by which a person is *oseh ḥesed im kono,* "acting kindly toward one's Creator."

THE HUMAN BEING:
BEARER OF DIVINE COMPASSION

Here I would like to offer an interpretation of an ancient question asked by the rabbis. "When God created the world," the Midrash asks, "did God do so by *middat ha-raḥamim,* the attribute of compassion, or by *middat ha-din,* the attribute of judgment?" The rabbis probably originally meant this question in moralistic terms: was it justice or mercy that filled the divine thought in the hour when humans were created? Is it the virtue of human justice or human compassion that makes the race worthy of creation? Both could be found somewhat wanting. But Jewish philosophers of a later era saw this debate in another way. Within it they couched their own question: Did God create the world out of loving free will, or out of necessity? Was there a real choice when God decided whether to create or not, the decision to do so being an affirmative act of will? Or does the emanation flow forth because it is of the nature of God to do good, divine goodness by definition requiring a flowing forth of the stream of life? The theology I propose certainly seems to follow the latter course. The world, or the garbing of the One in the garments of being, happens not because a person-God freely chooses to have it that way, but rather, because an inner logic or a built-in inner drive brings forth that process. But the Midrash goes on to answer that God first tried to create the world by *din,* or necessity, and when "He saw the world could not stand, he added to it the quality of compassion."

I would say that we humans are that "quality of compassion"; *we* are the vessels through which *raḥamim,* or compassion, is added to God's *din.* The flow of life as we experience it is morally blind. We Jews can give more than sufficient testimony to that fact in this generation. But as humans we are here to direct that flow of life, to lead the divine energy in the world in the direction of compassion. We affirm that compassion is divine, that it is the presence of Y-H-W-H within us that causes us to give, to love generously, and to care. In this way, we truly become the viceroy of Y-H-W-H on earth. In our generation, more than ever, we mortals are taking an active role in directing the flow of life. As we unravel aspects of the secrets of birth and death, those great keys that the rabbis saw as being in the hands of God alone are in fact being shared more and more in human–divine partnership. May we learn to handle them with wisdom and compassion!

It is as *bearers of compassion* that we become the partners of Y-H-W-H in Creation. The divine energy flows outward from the source, through the complex and multipronged evolutionary process, and into us, giving us an extra sense of charge and dynamic movement forward. We, by adding to it the insight and act of compassion, send it streaming *back* to the One, our gift in gratitude for the gift of existence itself.

Yod Heh. The first two letters of the holy name. The primal point and the womb of cosmic birth. The two of them create י״ה, a name all its own. "For by YaH God formed the worlds." From the point of view of nonhuman nature, the process is here complete. But for us humans, unique bearers of that long collective memory we call history, *Yod Heh* is only half a name. As soon as there is a human presence in Creation, there is history. And then, indeed, Creation is only part of the story, one that calls out to us in the form of language and calls on us to act. *Yod Heh* thus flows on to *Vav Heh*. Born of the deepest recesses of our humanity, our faith in Creation calls us to be present to Revelation and Redemption as well.

REVELATION

Y-H-W-H and Language

*V*av, the third letter of the divine name, represents a *drawing forth*. It lengthens the *Yod* and brings it into the world. *Yod,* the first letter, is just a point. A point lies at the border between existence and nonexistence, between being and nothingness. This is all we can say of existence at this early stage. In *Yod,* Divinity remains entirely hidden. *Heh,* the most primal field of feminine energy, then joins with the *Yod* and brings forth the universe in an act of cosmic birth. Now *Vav* returns to the *Yod* and lengthens it, drawing it forth in the form of language. It is the source of life become articulate, the primal *davar* ("thing"), now received by humanity as *davar* ("word"), the One as spoken word. The One as *Yod* is not–yet–thing. As *Heh* it is all–things–in–birth. Now in *Vav* it is manifest as *language*. This manifestation in the word is what allows the One to be known by the human mind, which thinks in the categories of words and language. *It is this apprehension of the One-become-word in the human mind that we call revelation.*

The reader will rise to protest. "We have already seen the two sides of the One! Stasis and movement, Y-H-W-H without and Y-H-W-H within, God 'before' Creation and God 'in' Creation, *sovev* and *memale,* emptiness and fullness, naught and all. What room can there possibly be for another category here? *Is not Creation itself sufficient revelation,* the One manifest throughout the world, 'renewing each day, constantly, the act of Creation'? What more could we need?"

Yod Heh is indeed a divine name on its own. Were our world simply that of nature, one not transformed for us by human consciousness and creativity, *YaH* alone would suffice. Adding the *Vav* to *Yod Heh* is a recognition of our human distinctiveness, our special status as *medabberim,* speaking, thinking, and conscious beings. The One as manifest in Creation, *Yod Heh,* belongs equally to all; it is part of human protoplasm in the same way that it is part of animal, plant, and rock. The human may recognize it, but does not own it in any distinctive way. In YaH-in-Creation we are part of the natural order. But now, with the addition of the *Vav,* that One enters in a wholly different way into the human mind; the all-pervasive presence is now *spoken* within us, and that can happen only to us creatures of speech. *God becomes word as we become human.*

In turning to address our people's ancient tale of Sinai from this theological perspective, we find ourselves turning doubly from the general to the specific. We turn both from the universal–natural to the specifically human, and from the universal–human to the specifically Jewish. *Yod* and *Heh* encompass all existence. *Vav* belongs to the human alone. Until now, we have been dealing with truths known and revealed to all humans, as discussed in the language of a renewed Judaism. Now we turn to the heart of Judaism itself.

BEFORE THE MOUNTAIN

We are beset by trembling as we approach Sinai, the mountain peak of Jewish faith. Here is the turning point between the revelation of Divinity and the response of humans. We cannot speak of one without the other. Divine voice and human voice are fully intertwined with one another, bound in embrace like the cherubim over the Ark. Divine speech is made accessible to us only through the human vessel, one that embodies it and hides it at once. Human languages are many, each of them bespeaking the divine encounter in its own voice; hiding–revealing the One in its own way. The divine life as manifest in the world is open to all and goes beyond the language of any tradition. The divine light shines on all without distinction; it is only the differences in our own cultural settings that make for religious difference, that receive, refract, and transmit the light through various symbolic vessels. But when we discuss human response to the divine reality, we can discuss only specifics. Humanity has responded to the reality that is God not in only one way. Here, the Oneness of God is refracted through the variety of human traditions, rites, prayers, and forms of expression.

Sinai indeed takes us to the heart of Jewish faith: it claims that there is communication from God to humans, and that such communication took place between Y-H-W-H and Moses and Israel at that mountain in the wilderness. Through this revelation, the will of God as manifest in Judaism becomes known. In one form or another, that claim pervades all of classical Judaism. It will be necessary here both to deny this claim and to affirm it. For some, undoubtedly, the denial will go too far. It may be that the theological position outlined here will be too distant for them from the simple notion of revelation they had in childhood. Others may find the views expressed here too dangerously humanistic, not providing sufficient basis for the distinctive claims of Judaism, and especially for *halakhah.* For yet another group of readers, the affirmation will undoubtedly be too strong. The theological tone of the views I express may sound to them too much like a real belief in revelation after all. I proceed from the premise of seeking a mature and believable Jewish faith, based on an ultimate commitment to a nondualistic vision of the universe. I seek to remain faithful to an understanding that the "portrait of the king" is a mirror of the self, and that each of our self-portraits is a mirror of the One. All the rest proceeds from here.

If revelation and commandment are the heart of Jewish faith, they are also the most difficult and "scandalous" claim made by the religious traditions of Israel. Taken at face value, they form the very essence of Jewish supernaturalism and seeming theological arbitrariness: God, the Creator of the universe, chooses at a particular moment in human history to reveal Himself uniquely to the Jewish people, addressing them in words and covenanting His eternal loyalty to them if they will accept His specific will as manifest in the practice of Judaism. Both mind and conscience reel at such a thought! What does it mean to say that God speaks? Is there, then, a divine voice, one that knows words, quite independent of language as a human creation? Does God speak to Israel in a language that Israel understands, commanding a Torah made up of laws, ethics, rites, and traditions that seem remarkably related to those of the pagan nations in whose midst Israel lives? Does the Creator of the universe (or the One within and without) have a will so specific that it concerns itself with details of Sabbath observance, proper preparation of sacrifices, and all the rest that will comprise the great codes of Jewish law? Can we imagine a God so arbitrary as to choose one nation, one place, and one moment in human history in which the eternal divine will was to be manifest for all time? Why should the ongoing traditions, institutions, and prejudices of the Western Semitic tribes of that era be visited on humanity as the basis for fulfilling the will of God? How can a God who visits only Israel deliver a message for all of humanity, especially for the more than half of humanity whose spiritual traditions have nothing to do with Sinai and its legacy? How can we attribute to Y-H-W-H, who is person only through our encounter, this sort of arbitrary willfulness? For these reasons and others, thinking Jews in our time, including many who seek a serious approach to questions of the spirit, balk at accepting the "yoke" of Sinai.

There are more than a few intimations in earlier Jewish literature telling us that we modern Jews are not the first to have difficulty with literal and dualistic views of revelation. A well-known midrash claims that God offered the Torah to each nation of the world, only to have it rejected, before coming to Israel. Each nation sought to know what the Torah demanded before accepting it, and each found some reason to reject it. Only Israel said *na'aseh ve-nishma* ("we will do and listen"). Only Israel agreed to receive Torah out of love for God, even before they heard its contents. This story is an ancient apologetic for the exclusiveness of Israel's claim. We are not the "chosen people," says this midrash, but merely the only people who were willing to choose God's Torah. The idea that God has been revealed to other nations, at least in historical action, if not in words, was already apparent to the prophets, even if it tended to be forgotten in later Judaism.

Human Understanding
and Divine Speech

The *nature* of divine speech has also been debated by philosophers and theologians throughout Jewish history. Each of the great theologies proposed by Jews in both medieval and modern times offered some theory of prophecy or revelation. The prophet is often depicted as a philosopher or contemplative, one whose mind is so open that it reaches beyond the borders of ordinary human understanding. For Maimonides and those who followed him, study and rigorous philosophic training are seen as part of the preparation necessary for the ultimate human experience. These serve to train consciousness, allowing the mind to expand in a way that enables it to receive the divine influx. When the intellectual and imaginative faculties are both fully attuned, a revelatory event is virtually assured. The ecstatic mystics who followed in Maimonides' path understood him to be saying that they, too, could achieve prophetic states, and they used various meditative techniques in hope of attaining prophecy. The Zohar claims that the only knowledge of God we can have is that which we imagine within our own heart.

In the mystical tradition, a variety of sources point to something beyond dualism. I have already referred to the ancient midrash that speaks of the seeker as being like an animal who wanders into the woods and finds a pond of water. Astonished, the animal looks down and sees "another" animal in the pond. All the prophets but Moses saw "through a darkened glass," explained by commentators as a glass with silvered backing, or a mirror. Prophetic revelation is the discovery of a deeper self. Some sources attribute revelation to a "higher" aspect of soul or consciousness that remains "above" when the soul enters the person at birth. It is the prophet's "other self" that speaks through the prophet's mouth, the portion or aspect of the soul that remains One with God, even after the person has become differentiated. Notwithstanding formal declarations to the contrary, there were some among the kabbalists, as well as the philosophers, who thought they could recreate prophecy with proper inner training.

Even the early rabbis, who are often depicted as quite literalist and naive in their views of revelation, offer us more than a few hints to the contrary. When Exodus 19:19 tells us that "Moses spoke and God responded in a voice," the rabbis add, "in the voice of Moses." This seems to say that the *only* voice heard at Sinai was that of Moses, sometimes speaking on his own, and sometimes possessed by the divine spirit. Rather than a "voice from heaven," there was the voice of a prophet transformed by an inner encounter that can only be characterized as "heaven." Thinking Jews over many centuries have debated how fully to refine the naive biblical depiction of Sinai and the experience of revelation.

The fact is that any sophisticated theory of revelation recognizes a moment in which the divine and human minds flow together and are not clearly separable from one another. Indeed, we use the word "mind" of the divine whole only by analogy with its human part. If Y-H-W-H is the noncorporeal essence of the universe, and mind or soul is the noncorporeal essence of the person, we *call* God the mind or soul of the universe. But this is not to claim that the functions are identical. Divinity embraces both body and soul. The noncorporeal essence and its garb are all one as part of being. God as Y-H-W-H knows no distinction between matter and spirit. But in seeking to comprehend revelation, we may speak of Y-H-W-H as cosmic mind, present in the depths of each human mind, and here impressing itself in a unique way upon consciousness. The universal One seeks out manifestation in the human, seeks to be known by this manifestation of its own self that is also, paradoxically, its "other." Its "seeking," or its "calling out," to that "other" is not of language. It is only the human that can make the divine articulate in words, since words themselves are a human invention. In fact, a more literal reading of Exodus 19:19 would render it, "Moses spoke and God responded *in thunder,*" as the contemporary translations indicate. *Y-H-W-H speaks in thunderclaps; it takes a Moses to translate God's thunder into words.*

If the divine and human are regarded as separate in the Jewish imagination, God living in "heaven" and humans on earth, revelation is the act that most overcomes this separation. Moses goes up to the top of Sinai, according to the Torah, and God also comes down upon the mountain (Exodus 19:3, 20). But then the entire top of Sinai is covered by thick cloud—as though to say that the border between the "upper" and "lower" realms is lost at that moment. Later accounts of the revelation are more fanciful and actually depict Moses as riding on the clouds, entering the heavenly realms, and holding on to God's Throne of Glory. Moses returns from the revelation still a human, but his face glows with the light of that encounter in which the uppermost limits of human spiritual attainment had been momentarily cast aside. He returns to the "world of separation" from an experience of transcendent unity, the Torah now "translated" within him. God's thunder and Moses' words are now one.

THE INNER MOUNTAIN

But the God who speaks in thunder is still the sky god, still the one who dwells in heaven and atop the highest peak. We are seeking a more fully *internalized* version of that foot-of-the-mountain experience. Earlier, we suggested turning the high mountain into a deep well. Using either of these metaphors (for the mountain, too, can exist within), we try to understand revelation as the most profound of inner experiences. Seen this way, Moses' experience has much in common with the creative act, the inner mental activity of the artist, the musical composer, the mathematician, and others, along with the religious figure. The core experience of creativity reaches a depth that necessarily contains an element of mystery. Creative people often describe this as a place within them where the concentration of inner energy allows the ordinary self to be overwhelmed, and something "other" to take its place. We are talking about an inner straining of the human mind to the breaking point—but rather than a break*down* that leads to madness or confusion, we envision a break*through* that leads to new creative achievements. This may come in the form of an insight that did not exist before, a flash of intuition that is instantaneously translated into the medium in which the creator works: into music, into mathematical formula, into words. The creative energy, like the divine light, is undifferentiated. Only the tools and mind-set that lead one to it draw on that mysterious inner reserve and direct each to be creative in a specific way. (The rabbis say that at Sinai the very senses were confused, and Israel "saw the audible and heard the visible." We can only imagine a state of creative elation from which Einstein would return with a symphony, and Beethoven with a mathematical formula!) *At this rung of human inner experience, lines between "creativity," "discovery," "inspiration," and "revelation" are impossible to draw.* The language we have for drawing such fine distinctions belongs to a level of consciousness other than that at which these inner events occur. The free flow of inner energies that characterizes such moments does not admit clear borders between "mine" and "Thine."

When that stretching involves the soul, or the human capacity to love and tremble in awe, as well as the mind, the human capacity to understand, then the creative–inspirational–revelatory event takes on a religious character. It becomes a *life-transforming* event. Out of it may emerge a vision of a new or redeemed social order as well. The human striving for revelation involves a full extension of the emotional, intellectual, and moral life as one. We Jews assert that Moshe Rabbenu—either historically or as a symbol of the ancient Jewish people—was a person who had such experience. The religion of ancient Israel, as embodied symbolically in that moment of Sinai, continues to represent for us the result of one of the great human encounters with Divinity. For us as Jews—existentially speaking—it is the greatest such encounter of all time. Indeed, *it is the only one we know.* We understand that there may exist other such encounters as well, and they may take different forms. But these are not existentially open to us; they are not *ours.* True participation in a spiritual language requires the whole of the human heart. Each heart can speak only one such language. Our heart is given wholly to this one.

While we recognize that there may be others, we cannot know them, cannot "set them upon our heart."

But what was the *content* of that moment at Sinai? If revelation is to be analogized to the experience of creativity or discovery, there needs to be a "something" that is revealed. What was it that Moses or Israel discovered, created, had revealed? Moses is the one who saw beyond the darkened glass, who looked into the brightness. What did he bring back from that indescribable moment? Was it something like the great piece of music, or the scientific breakthrough, a result of revelation creativity as we might understand it? Yes, but articulating it is not simple. All of our Torah, in the broadest sense, may be called an ongoing, stammering, and always inadequate attempt at this articulation.

Out of Sinai comes Y-H-W-H, the reality and the word. Sinai offers Y-H-W-H as the singular divine presence that pervades all the world and reaches beyond it in ways we humans are not given to fully understand. This reality, Sinai tells us, is accessible to human beings at the greatest moments of their lives. The same ecstatic presence that filled the hearts of Israel as they walked proudly out of Egypt, the same presence that was to so fill the Tent of Meeting that no person was able to enter it, could be found in human life, both for individuals and for the nation, again and again in the future. *Ehyeh Asher Ehyeh,* "I shall be that I shall be," is interpreted by the rabbis to mean "I shall be with you again as I was with you then." The manifestation of Y-H-W-H that happened in Israel's hearts and minds at Sinai is an assurance that such manifestation does not happen then alone. Revelation reveals the *possibility* of revelation, not just that once, but whenever the human heart and mind are open to it. Israel further comes to understand that this presence that offers inspiration to be free ("the revelation at the Sea") and guidance to the one who seeks it ("the revelation at the Mountain") was there also before the existence of our world itself, and will be there even after our world is gone. The name Y-H-W-H is the very core of this revelation, as bearer of the insight that God was-is-will be, containing all of time in eternal presence.

TORAH AS THE NAME OF GOD

In saying that the name of God is the core of revelation, we are presenting a theology that is at once entirely traditional and highly radical. "I am Y-H-W-H," God says to Moses, "I appeared to Abraham, to Isaac, and to Jacob as El Shaddai, but by My name Y-H-W-H I was not known to them" (Exodus 6:2–3). The revelation to Moses begins with God's name, both in this passage and in the Ten Commandments. The kabbalists spoke of the entire Torah as the name of God, or sometimes of the divine name as the essence of all language.

What is it, in fact, that was spoken by God to Israel at Sinai? The tradition contains both maximalist and minimalist views on this key question. The Bible's claim in this regard is fairly obvious: "Y-H-W-H spoke all these words, saying" is followed by the ten commandments (Exodus 20:1). But some of the early rabbis expand this claim vastly and include the entire Torah within the scope of revelation at the moment of Sinai. (They even discuss whether Moses at Sinai wrote the last eight verses of Deuteronomy, beginning "Moses the servant of Y-H-W-H died there," some admitting that Joshua added these as a postscript, while others insist that Moses, hearing them spoken by God, wrote them down with his tears.) Their later followers expanded the claim even further, insisting that the Oral Torah (including Mishnah and Talmud) was from Sinai as well. The next expansion of this position was given voice in a saying attributed to Rabbi Joshua ben Levi: "Everything a faithful student is ever to say was already given to

Moses at Sinai." Here, the scope of revelation is broadened to infinity, encompassing within it (and thus granting legitimacy to) every proper interpretation of Torah to be offered down to the end of time. The final maximalist view is that of the Zohar: "There is *nothing* that has not been hinted at in the Torah."

Thus far the maximalists. But there is also a minimalist reading on the question of what was said and heard at Sinai. One midrash claims that Israel in fact heard only two commandments out of the mouth of the divine Dynamis—"I am Y-H-W-H your God," and "You shall have no other gods beside Me"—when they interrupted the revelation out of their great fear. It was at this point that they said to Moses, "You speak with us and we will listen, but let not Y-H-W-H speak with us, lest we die" (Exodus 20:16). This would mean that all the rest of revelation comes to Israel through the mind as well as the mouth of the prophet, shaped by his own translator's imagination, and only these two utterances are, in the fullest sense, the "word of God." Here, awareness of Y-H-W-H and the prohibition of idolatry in all its forms are described as the basis of all Judaism. The philosopher Franz Rosenzweig apparently at one point considered a still more restricted formulation, debating whether God had spoken even the first *word* of the commandments ("I am"). All the rest is Israel's commentary, elaboration, and response. Another radically minimalist view is to be found in the teachings of a hasidic master. This view has God speaking only the first *letter* of the first word. That letter, aleph, is in itself silent. God speaks only the great silence; the Divine is a silent womb that contains all of language within it.

In seeing the name as the content of revelation, we draw together the maximalist and minimalist views as ends of a circle. *All God says is that which cannot be spoken, the pronounce-ment of the unpronounceable word.* But this word is filled to overflowing with the energy of Being. It contains within it all the power of Creation that it bore when it was first spoken as *yehi* ("let there be"). Thus it allows us to bring *all words* to Sinai. Revelation is that which makes for *leshon ha-kodesh:* it allows for the sanctification of human speech. The name is the divine self as language; that which Y-H-W-H "gives" at Sinai is nothing other than Y-H-W-H, for "the blessed Holy One and Torah are One." This is the truth of Sinai as I understand it. To this indeed all else is commentary and response.

Revelation and the Inward Journey

This claim for a point of inner contact between human mind and universal Self is in need of yet another set of quotation marks, which the reader will note are being used so generously at this point in our discussion. The word "between" also needs this designation, for the true nature of the mind's encounter with the One is not to be seen as a meeting of "self" and "other." The human–divine encounter *is more like the breaking down of a wall than like the building of a bridge.* It is a discovery that there is no chasm, rather than a claim that the gap can be traversed. Finally, it is the realization that the wall itself was illusory, and the sense of separation lay only in our own unreadiness to know the deeper truth.

The claim is not being made for Moses alone. The Judaism of today's seeker is not that of the one who stands faithfully at the base of the mountain (or the edge of the well!), waiting for the leader to return and proclaim the divine message. It is, rather, a Judaism that seeks to go *with* Moses—or Akiva, who is seen by the tradition as a latter-day heavenly voyager—to those heights or depths, and to participate in Israel's ongoing attempt to articulate that encounter.

But our claim goes still further. *Every* human journey contains within it something of Moses' trek up that mountainside; every human attempt at making meaning, at understanding the purpose of human existence, at rejecting cynicism in quest of truth, has something of Sinai within it. Whenever we assert—by deed as well as by word—that life is not absurd, that accident and emptiness are not our only lot, we are climbing up God's mountain. Believe as we may that it is we who are making for life's meaning, we who are retrieving human dignity from the abyss of chaos, the religious mind sees such activity as *response* rather than as human creativity alone. We give meaning all its forms, but the need to do so is an act of responding to the divine image cast into our deepest human selves. We perform the act of naming, calling the divine by the names chosen by our tradition. But that need to name exists in us because we are called upon to do so by the One within.

We further assert that all of us Jews, in all generations, as the story says, are there with Moses, or—to say it in less mythical terms—the Jewish people there made an all-time commitment, a covenant to remain faithful forever to the reality of that moment. Each of us, as we lay claim to our spiritual heritage, may return to intimate communion with that ever-resounding event at Sinai, formative of the Jewish spirit for all generations. It is in this sense that I understand the covenantal aspect of Sinai and of Judaism as a whole.

THE ROLE OF COVENANT: A REINTERPRETATION

The God-initiated covenant of the Bible, a pillar of classical Judaism's self-understanding, cries out for reinterpretation in our day. In a Jewish faith where God is not "wholly other," and where the "will" of God is far from a simple notion, "covenant" cannot be understood in its most obvious sense. The religious language we have inherited speaks of a God who chooses Israel from among all nations to receive the single revelation as manifest in Torah. It is God's "election of Israel," to use the classic term, that initiates the covenant. But God as *chooser* is a highly anthropomorphized notion of Y-H-W-H. Once we see the very depiction of God as person to be the result of human projection onto the universe, divine choosing will also have to be recognized as projection, as *Israel's way of asserting that it stands as a people in a unique relationship with the Divine.*

It is *we* who make this covenant, we who, in the person of Moses, dash half the blood of a sacramental offering over the altar—representing God—and pour the other half over ourselves, binding ourselves in an act of eternal commitment to the One of Sinai. In doing so, the Jewish people performs an act of eternal living commitment, forging a link between this event and all Jewish generations to come. It is in this sense that we continue to speak of Sinai as covenant. It is we who at Sinai declare our undying devotion to the universal ever-flowing and yet unchanging One.

Is the covenant then a one-sided affair? What does covenant mean if there are not two partners between whom the commitment is made? Here again, the religious language we speak—that of "self" and "other"—has to be read anew in the light of our nondualistic point of view. If relationship with God is more like breaking down a wall (or seeing through a veil) than it is like building a bridge across a chasm, covenant, too, becomes a commitment to *keeping faith with the deepest Self that is manifest within us.* It is a decision to live in such a way that allows this One to be revealed to others through us. Covenant is our willingness to be a channel, to serve as a conduit of God's presence to those with whom we live. "Israel exists in order to open paths, to light up the ways, and to kindle lamps—to raise everything up, so that all be One."

Once again, we may read our projection of covenant "from God's point of view" as well. The divine light extends to all peoples, as it does to each individual soul. Israel has made the commitment of devoting itself to that light and bringing it into the world, making itself and its history a channel for divine presence. The choice to do so may be Israel's, but this act of self-dedication (that the Jewish people has called "choosing") may still be seen as one from which Y-H-W-H is by no means absent. Is it not the God within us who chooses to hear the voice of God? Is the voice of Israel that says *na'aseh venishma* ("We will do and listen"), not also one in which Y-H-W-H is speaking?

The task of religion is twofold. To return for a moment to the vertical metaphor, we would say that religion has both to take us to the heights of human attainment and to raise up the valleys that lie between them, to make for peak moments in our lives, but also to ensure that we do not sink too low when those special moments seem far from us. Religion is both charismatic and institutional, to say it in other words. Its language coaxes forth in us those peak experiences that become the core of the individual's and the community's commitments. But the other no less serious, and perhaps more difficult, task of religion is building institutions that will allow us to shape the rest of our lives in faithfulness to those charismatic moments. *Le-ma'an tizkeru,* "so that you remember," is the way we say this in Hebrew, and it is the basis for all of form in religion. In youth, we are impatient with religion for being overly institutional and not leaving enough room for the pure freedom that seems to be required by the spiritual energy churning within us. As we mature, we come to understand that religion faces the great task of uplifting *ordinary* life, the realms of work, family, and humdrum existence, of bringing these, too, into the spectrum of spiritual awareness. Only the discipline provided by institutional structure (dare I say "*halakhah*"?) can perform that task.

The Jewish people throughout its history has accepted the task of forming a *communal* religious existence and creating a *civilization* that stands in response to the event at Sinai. This is what I mean by *Kabbalat ha-Torah,* "accepting the Torah." What we accept is the reality that divinity is present to humans, in human language and human institutions, and the challenge to create a society that embodies this presence. *We are no less charged with that task today than we were thousands of years ago.* For this reason, the civilization the Jewish people creates in this act of response, by the very definition of its task, has to evolve continually. The nature of standing in God's presence in this generation after the Holocaust, in this generation of nuclear weapons, and in this generation of threatened ecological disaster, is clearly different from the task of standing in God's presence in the *shtetl* a hundred years ago or in *Erets Yisra'el* in ancient times. As the nature of that task changes, the way the Jewish people responds must continually grow and change.

REVELATION AND TORAH

*O*ur written Torah *represents the Jewish people's first attempt to create such a civilization.* In it, we made our first transition from wordless revelation, through prophetic speech, to the creation of a holy society, from the stillness and passivity of becoming aware to the realization and embodiment of that awareness in social form. As such, Torah is the basis of all further attempts. We look upon it not as the specifically revealed will of God, and not as a body of binding legislation, but rather, as the ancient and powerful root of our people's civilization. Certainly, it still has a *hold* upon us: not a binding hold of law, but a hold the way one's deepest and most ancient psyche continues to have a powerful grasp on a person's actions throughout life. The Torah represents the psychic source from which we all come. We respond to it in deep and personal ways. That response includes love and deep loyalty; at times it may also include rebellion or anger. But Torah, all of Torah, is present throughout the continuing evolution of Judaism.

But this explanation of the relationship between revelation and Torah, a wordless or nearly wordless revelation to which Torah is Israel's historic human response, does not seem quite adequate. Are the words and religious institutions of Torah, then, *only* human? Would we say *merely* human? Is there no divine presence about them? Let us remember once again that we are operating in a universe where the lines between the Divine and the human are less than rigid. Can we not say that the *tselem Elohim,* the image of God, is reflected in the religious institutions that human beings create? If we are a part of Divinity and bear its presence within us, the Jewish people (or any other religious community) over centuries has the power to sanctify, which is to say "bring the divine presence into," the essential forms of its religious life for all its descendants. Could this be what Mordecai Kaplan meant when he spoke of the *mitsvot* as *sancta* of the Jewish people? The essential forms of tradition are indeed holy and must be followed, not because God dictated them from the mountain top, but because the Jewish people, using its own sacred energy, declared them holy to its God. This is reflected in the language of our holiday blessings: "*mekadesh Yisra'el ve . . .*" "sanctifying Israel and . . ."; the sanctification of the holiday takes place through Israel. I would apply this model to the entirety of our religious expression.

To say it somewhat differently, and perhaps more mystically, I would offer the following. The Jewish people has invested the forms of its devotional life, including the words of prayer, the cycle of the calendar, its sacred music, and even tales and commentaries that have been told and retold, with boundless emotional and spiritual energy over many generations. I believe that the power of this *kavvanah* is never lost. The intensity with which a form is used as a vessel of spiritual life grows and builds through each generation of devotion to it. The treasury of spiritual riches borne by the words of prayer or the form of offering gains in ever-increasing richness over time. A latter-day Jew, especially one coming from outside the tradition, who opens to that form, may discover the tremendous riches of *kavvanah* that lie waiting within it. The Jewish people has both created and accepted these forms in love. That love is never lost or diminished, but is only hidden until we discover it again. The forms may not have been *given* by God from Sinai, but they are *what we bring to the mountain;* we invest them and forever associate them with the holiness we encounter there.

Of course, the dangers of institutional religion are also ever present. Overinstitutionalization can indeed lock out the charismatic core that the form was created to preserve. There are those who become loyal to the forms alone. Traditional Judaism contains within it a preoccupation with the detail of form that is truly overwhelming. Surely there have always been those for whom this preoccupation serves as a positive reminder of the true content. But over the centuries, as this ever-extending passion for correct performance in each detail has been allowed to run rampant, Judaism for many has become a religion of devotion to performance, or commitment to religious law, that stands in great danger of forgetting its own spiritual center. The early hasidic masters certainly knew this, and overemphasis on institutional religion, rather than on its sacred core, was what the hasidic revival set out to correct. As hasidism felt the need to take on the mantle of defending tradition, the character of Hasidism changed. It, too, became overly devoted to the protection of outward form, including the specific outward form of hasidic tradition. The tension between *keva* and *kavvanah,* fixed form and inner content, is an ongoing struggle within Judaism, as it is in traditional religion throughout the world.

REVELATION, WILL, AND LAW

What room does such a view of revelation and its relationship with *mitsvah* leave for the role of law in Judaism? The content of revelation is the divine name or self, the personal face of Being. This may be spiritually fulfilling, but we seem to be left quite entirely without a notion of specific divine will. Is it not the will of God that has always served as the theological underpinning for the authority of Jewish law? We understand that *halakhah* properly means "the path," and that "law" is a somewhat unfortunate mistranslation. But the codification of human behavior into categories of "permitted" and "forbidden" in accord with the will of God is surely highly characteristic of classical Judaism, and remains the dividing line between Orthodoxy and all non-Orthodox forms of Judaism in our day.

This description of our situation is to a large degree accurate; the theology offered here is clearly that of a non-Orthodox Jew. What you are reading is a heterodox mystical theology of Judaism. I do see a divine intent or will in the life force, as manifest in the evolutionary process, and especially in the ongoing striving toward consciousness. This is not "will" in our highly personalistic human sense, but a striving inherent in the very existence and evolution of the universe. Our human response to (or participation in!) this "will" is to be found in the affirmation of life, in recognizing the divine image in ourselves and in others, in acts of kindness—primarily in the human community but embracing all living creatures—and in the nurturing of awareness. This response requires human societies to create such forms, including legal institutions, domestic arrangements, and so forth, that will embody this will. The same is true of forms of worship and religious discipline. If awareness of the One is to be cultivated in the human community, ordered forms of spiritual expression will have to exist. In this sense, we may say that religion is *our human fulfillment of the divine will or purpose.* The need for human societies to create religious forms is rooted, in this sense, in "the will of God" or the desire of the One for balanced and lasting self-manifestation. In another way, I also believe that *teshuvah,* the turning of all things toward their root in God, may be seen as a reflection of divine will in the creaturely world. The turning of all things toward their source in the One is rooted in existence itself. We will discuss this further in the coming chapter.

I recognize that none of this quite gets us to the point of explicit divine authority for the specific forms created by the Jewish people. In this gap lies the unorthodoxy of my position. To be sure, we Jews believe in the importance of law in the conduct of human life. When it comes to those areas governed by civil and criminal codes, Judaism stands firmly for the notion of the rule of law, with or without the convention of divine origin. Our questions about law refer primarily to the appropriateness of legal categories to the sphere of worship or religious devotion, but do not touch the importance or value of law itself. I do not know a God who "commands" specific religious behavior or forms of worship. I also believe that our way of response to the divine within the universe needs to grow and evolve with our history. But it is also clear to me that my very recognition of the divine image in my fellow human, and the need to sustain that recognition (even in his, her, or my least elevated moments), will take us right back to the need for law in the conduct of human affairs.

One of the earliest and most interesting exponents of the Torah, but whose work was lost to Jews for many centuries, is the philosopher Philo of Alexandria. Writing in Greek just over two thousand years ago, Philo was the first to attempt to understand the Torah traditions in terms of Greek categories of thought. Philo speaks of a notion of natural law, an eternal way of wisdom that teaches humans how to live in harmony with the natural world. This law, he says, was known to the ancients. When the Torah claims that Abraham observed God's law before the Torah was given, Philo tells us that the law our patriarch followed was in fact the natural law of the universe. It was his own inner wisdom that taught him to live in harmony with the universe. This affinity for natural law was the "original" Judaism. The Torah as we have it is Israel's attempt (Philo would say Moses' attempt) to approximate this natural law by means of human legislation. The Torah contains within it such important measures as protection for the weak, humane treatment of animals, and regard for the natural environment. The Torah lends us a sense of responsibility for ourselves, our families, and especially those less fortunate than we are. It repeats the law of nature "in human language." Torah is a way of bringing us to live in harmony with God's own law.

Rabbinic Judaism also contains within it an ancient principle that is quite close to the notion of natural law. According to the rabbis, seven commandments were given to the children of Noah after the flood. These include the prohibitions against murder, incest and adultery, theft, idolatry, and blasphemy, the injunction to establish courts of justice, and the injunction against dismemberment of living animals for food. These universal moral commandments are incumbent upon all human individuals and societies. With the latitude of interpretation and extension offered by our tradition, I believe we could continue to support the notion of the seven Noahide commandments as a basis for universal morality.

There is no question that the written Torah was a document of progressive social legislation in its time, as it was one of great spiritual and moral insight. The rabbis continued in this evolution of Torah, adding such refinements as the virtual abolition of the death penalty, the protection of women in divorce, the replacement of retribution by the payment of damages, and countless other refinements of moral legislation. *This process remains for us paradigmatic of that which we need to create.* For us Jews in Diaspora, the promulgation of humane legislation is generally something we do as members of the general society, however inspired by our Judaism. In the creation of a Jewish society in Israel, the Jewish people is given the tremendous opportunity and challenge of creating a legal system and a moral code that reflect both its roots in the prior history of Judaism and the best of contemporary moral sensibilities. This is not an easy task, as witnessed by the constant struggles in Israel over the place of Jewish law in the legal and institutional life of that society.

Judaism in its next manifestation will continue to need *halakhah.* This is simply to say that Judaism, like any religious tradition, will have to be defined and recognizable by forms of praxis, and cannot afford to let itself be dissipated into proclamation of theological or moral vagaries alone. Though it will not be justified as divine will in the literal sense, this *halakhah* can become the bearer of divine presence, the *davar shebi-kedushah,* in our lives. This new *halakhah,* rather than viewed as the specific will of God, will be understood as a human–divine embodiment, created by Israel, but in which real holiness is contained. Form as bearer of mysterious content, the outer as the needed vehicle to contain and convey the inner, will remain a vital part of Judaism in the future as it has been in the past. Our understanding of the relationship between outer and inner may shift and we may come to describe the origins of our sacred forms in new ways. But the need for them remains no less real than it has ever been.

In the preceding chapter, we have discussed some areas of this old–new *halakhah* as it relates to a theology of Creation. As we turn to do the same for revelation, I recognize the vast difference between our approach and that of tradition. In the past, the entirety of Torah and the Commandments were linked to revelation. Whatever other reasons or meanings might be found in the *mitsvot,* there was an ultimate ground in Judaism that demanded they all be fulfilled because they are the Creator's will. This is where all modern non-Orthodox Judaisms seriously diverge from their classical antecedents. Still, I believe there are halakhic implications to our faith in Sinai and revelation that I have articulated here, as there are to faith in Creation, and indeed to many other tales that we bear as Jews and tell from one generation to the next.

THE PERSONAL PATH:
ACCEPTING THE YOKE

The relationship between the memory of Sinai and our ever-evolving religious lives as Jews is not a simple one. There *is* divinity to be discovered within the *mitsvot*, but this is not the divinity of a commanding God who insists on their proper performance. Judaism *is* a way of reaching inward and outward toward the One, but a way sanctified by generations of those who walked along the path, rather than by divine fiat. *The light that lies hidden within our Torah, made up of the countless points of love and devotion placed there by our ancestors, is also the hidden light of Y-H-W-H.*

Is it then *imperative* that Jews seek out this light? Does the God who has dwelt within the hearts of so many generations, and who has been given expression through these forms, become an immanent *metsaveh*, a "commanding one," who will stand behind the *mitsvot* as the indwelling embodiment of religious authority? I find myself to be rather close to this position, but I am not ready to assert it in any but the most personal and subjective ways.

In my own religious life, I have come to recognize the need for *submission* to God as a part of religious devotion. I fought long and hard against this aspect of religious life, but I now, perhaps with long-delayed maturity, have come to accept it. I believe there is no room for God—however defined—in our lives until we can overcome our own willfulness. To thus submit, to "negate your will before God's will," is essential to accepting the covenant as I have described it, the readiness to serve as a channel for divine presence in the world.

In Judaism, this submission, usually described as *kabbalat ol malkhut shamayim* ("accepting the yoke of divine rule"), is joined to *kabbalat ol mitsvot* ("accepting the yoke of commandments"). For myself, I recognize the necessity of this link, the sense that religious awareness only becomes constant in life through the regularity of religious discipline. But I also remain constantly aware of the pitfalls of submission as a religious value. It can lead to the cultivation of overly-submissive personality. Some expressions of submission, in our tradition as well as elsewhere, border on self-hatred. Most seriously, from a devotional point of view, the emphasis on submission may be at the expense of the true joy and exultation that are the heart of religious awareness (how many *shaharit*-daveners I have seen who do not even seem to notice God's sunrise!). I turn to religious language to express the fullness of my heart. Let me be wary that religion itself not serve to diminish that fullness and its joy.

Here, the non-Orthodoxy of my theology is critical to my religious life. Because I know of the human role in the origin of the commandments, and because I know that all human creations are fallible, I never hand myself over entirely to them. I know that they are but a means, and an often arbitrary one, to the greater end of spiritual awareness. Out of my love for our ancestors and the divine spirit that dwelt within them, I choose to live in faithfulness to the religious discipline they created. I will do so wherever this discipline does not bring me into conflict with more deeply held religious principles: awareness that Y-H-W-H is One, manifest throughout the world, recognizing all humans as bearers of the divine image, and the seven Noahide commandments, as I understand them. Each day I seek to affirm anew this commitment to the *mitsvot* as my religious language, to keep it an act of faith ever chosen in freedom. I, too, must cross the Sea each day before I can renew the covenant.

I am helped in this struggle with authority in religion by the very *helplessness* of God. The One who is present in these *mitsvot* is really no longer the frightening commander on the mountaintop. I thank the ever self-revealing Y-H-W-H for the gifts of biblical scholarship and historical study of religion that have helped to break the excessive yoke of that sort of religious authority, making our generation a post- rather than a pre-modern one. The Presence that remains within the forms is the still, small voice of our people's deepest inner self. The God I know is a divinity that cannot act or be realized in the human world at all, except through human actions. Knowing full well that I live in an age of choice and freedom, one in which I can opt to leave the domain of this religious choice at any moment, I choose to remain "at home" with the life rhythms of the Jewish people. In doing so, I let myself hear that pleading voice of the One that has so long inhabited these traditions, and that asks not to be abandoned by yet another one of Israel's children.

Such an imperative is, of course, an entirely personal one. I share it with the reader without advocacy. I have seen too much of the dark and dangerous side of religion to dare prescribe submission for anyone but myself. Though I take delight in others who join me on this path, I will not permit myself to become anyone else's surrogate "commander."

SINAI AND LANGUAGE

In turning to the more specific *halakhah* of revelation, we are asking: "To what does the presence of Y-H-W-H in language obligate us?" What claim is made on our lives by this connection between the divine and the verbal, by this drawing forth of the hidden *Yod* into the *Vav* of speech? What demand upon us is made by the specific form taken by our tale, that of the people standing before God at Sinai?

The claim that divinity can enter human language, or that the indescribable One of Being, utterly beyond words and language, can enter into human speech through the agency of the word Y-H-W-H, is both to elevate human language itself to a new level of respect and to make tremendous demands upon it. It grants that language can, after all, transcend itself and serve as a vehicle for articulating states of consciousness and levels of reality that seem beyond its ken. The word Y-H-W-H is here seen as a token of the promise that language can be reborn in symbolic form, ready to embody heights and depths unknown to its prior ordinary discursive state.

The ability of language to reach into the human soul in such a way is both powerful and dangerous. Our century has seen too much of the abuse of myth and symbol as means of control over others for us to regard such claims for language benignly. If we assert that language has such power, this assertion must immediately be accompanied by a statement of commitment to what our sages called *brit ha-lashon,* "the covenant of the tongue," that is attributed precisely to Sinai.

The memory of Sinai demands of us that we use language in pure and sacred ways: that its powers not be used to manipulate or to pervert the truth. We must not use language to set one human community and its symbols over another, and we must especially remain ever aware that the same power of language that brings us to the gates of divinity has been used to dehumanize and bring whole peoples (including ourselves) to the gates of hell. Language must be used to bring us back to the One.

In our daily lives as well, we must come to understand that language is a precious and sacred vessel. Its power to draw us together in community—especially through sharing the language of prayer—is great. So too is its power of destruction. Malicious talk divides people from one another so deeply that the rabbis compare it to the shedding of blood. To know Y-H-W-H as Torah is to know the power of words and to devote ourselves to *leshon hakodesh,* to the purity of language.

The faith in potency of language, expressed in our opening to Y-H-W-H in revelation, carries over also into our commitment to verbal prayer. As Jews, we proclaim that we can find the divine presence in words, phrases, and sacred texts handed down to us by our ancestors. This is what it means to lay claim to a spiritual heritage that is conveyed to us mostly in language. We now take that same language and use it to give, rather than to receive. Into it we place our own deepest feelings of love and awe, of affirmation and doubt, of joy and terror. These we offer, a gift wrapped in the garb of sacred speech, to the One in whose presence we stand always.

SINAI AND STUDY

Faith in Sinai also commits us to a life of study. Judaism is a process of ongoing commentary. To be a Jew is to be a student. To be a self-affirming Jew is to love and study Torah. It is no small matter that the rabbis considered study equal in value to all the other *mitsvot* combined as one. We are a people devoted to a text. *Yisra'el ve-oraita had hu;* Israel and Torah are one. We can affirm this fully without denying the human origins of the Torah. We can celebrate it along with recognizing the fallibility of the text, along with agonizing over its moral imperfections, its ancient, rather than modern, sensibilities. A fallible text is one all the more in need of commentary, our way of bringing our past into the present before we hand it on to those who will create the future.

To be sure, the text has grown over the centuries. In the narrowest sense, our text is still the written Torah, those five books we read, study, and comment on in the synagogue each week. But that which was once commentary has now come to be included within text: Talmud and Midrash, *aggadah* and *halakhah, kabbalah* and hasidic tales and teachings are, in the broader sense, a part of our text. Jewish poetry and music, the writings of philosophers and the creations of artisans, woven fabrics for Torah curtains and elaborate towers for havdalah spice—all of these are part of the text we may choose to study. So too is the ongoing history of Israel; the lives led by Jewish men and women (the latter were largely excluded from the literary tradition) over the centuries are also a part of our "text," that to which we offer commentary by our own words and our own lives.

It is, after all, that historical *contextuality,* that living "with the text" that places us within the chain of tradition, that makes our generation a contributor to the sum of what will be passed on to the future. We do this faithfully only as we submit ourselves to the role of student, *as we are willing to allow ourselves to be shaped by the text as we have received it and made it our own.* The unchanging text serves as the counterpoint to our constant evolution and development. Yes, Judaism *must* grow and change in every age. This is true of both *halakhah* and *aggadah.* They need to keep faith with the life experience of the Jewish people at each moment in their history. But Judaism also contains a clear fixed point. Each generation struggles with the text, the *same* text, transformed and brought to life by interpretation, but itself never changing. As we struggle to add to tradition, to reshape it for each new generation, the text is also given a chance at reshaping us, at making a real demand on the way we think and live. It is only insofar as we have been faithful students that we will be good teachers. Tradition is a precious and fragile commodity in our age. We bear it carefully, adding to it of our own, to be sure, but not seeking entirely to bend it to our will, lest it break in our hands.

But our commitment to Torah study must be understood in a broader context as well. In a traditionally dualistic Western religious system, the need for Torah is quite apparent. The God who created humans in this world and has a specific will for human behavior would not be so cruel as to abandon us without telling us the law. How could we *not* commit ourselves to eternal study of God's own word? But in the theology I outline here, why do we need Torah to know God or to live the good life? If God is manifest in the world, study the world! If Divinity is in all of being, study astronomy, botany, or zoology—but why Torah?

Let me add here that I fully agree that Judaism in the past has been overly bookish. The turning away from nature as the great testimony to Y-H-W-H, which was still essential to our religious life in Biblical times, toward a religion where God was known only through the world of books and commentaries, was a terrible narrowing of the Jewish soul. This is being rectified by the generations of Jews who have returned to the land in Erets Yisra'el. We Diaspora Jews have been slower to learn this lesson.

But God is manifest in the human mind and spirit *as well as* in birds, trees, and human love. God is there in the human longing to comprehend and unite with Divinity. This stretching forth of mind and soul to that which is most deeply within us is an essential part of religion's value. The history of this seeking within the human race is a vital part of the story of Y-H-W-H. *Human faith itself is as much testimony to Y-H-W-H as are sunsets, seas, or mountains.* The history of the quest for God and for a God-inspired way of life among our people is a part of that story that we Jews alone can tell. We are obligated today, as always, to "tell it to our children." We are also obligated to preserve it as a part of the much-needed spiritual heritage of all humanity. In order to build a Judaism that will be of deep meaning to Jews in the future, we need to drink deeply of the teachings of the Jewish past. The religious value of Torah study is a seeking out of the ways in which the divine presence has been manifest in the Jewish people since the most ancient times. Its meaning changes, as it must, but it is still Torah.

Sinai and Community

Sinai was an experience of the entire people, a *communal* transformation, rather than that of an individual. When Israel arrived at the mountain, say the rabbis, they encamped there (the verb used is in the singular) "with a single heart"; only then were they ready to receive the word of God. Our religious language is that of community; it is *we* who stand before You, *we* who have sinned, and so forth. To live in faith with Sinai is to love and embrace the entire Jewish people. It is also to seek and build community, a grouping of like-thinking and like-living Jews whose collectivity will serve as a bridge between the individual and *klal Yisra'el,* the whole Jewish people.

We Jews who are still in the process of reclaiming our Judaism and returning to tradition in one way or another often think we do so as the result of our own individual odysseys, life experiences, and struggles that seem to us entirely private and idiosyncratic. But as we identify again with Judaism, we begin to find ourselves living richly in the context of the Jewish people, past, present, and future. Our role in linking the generations becomes a crucial part of our identity. We know too that *ahavat Yisra'el,* a love and compassionate caring for our fellow Jews, is a part of this heritage to which we return. There is no Judaism without Jews, and this is no mere tautology. Our religion is that of a people; there is no reclaiming the silent sounds or the holy moment of Sinai without reclaiming also as our own the *people* of Sinai, distanced as they may seem from the foot of that sacred mountain. Yes, the God we know is universal, and the divine image is there in every human. But there is also a strong place in our tradition to celebrate particularity, to stand close with those who share our history and, as we have been shown so strongly in our times, our *destiny,* as well as the special traditions we have inherited or chosen. This love extends to all Jews, including those with whom we have even the deepest theological or moral disagreements. It is as members of the same extended family that we love one another enough to argue, that we care enough to want to convince one another to mend our ways.

Somewhere in the course of living in community, we come to see that the journey is not an isolated one any more. As we build our own individual families in a communal context, or as we share in the broader "family" of community itself, we find that we have come *home* from the long wandering that so characterizes our contemporary society, home to our ancestors (whether biological or adopted), home to the Jewish people. Ultimately, we begin to see this process of odyssey and return as something more than individual, as belonging to the history of Jews in our day, so many of whom are seeking ways to reclaim our tradition. The decision to find our way as Jews, rather than to turn to the many other life paths that stretch before us in this age of seemingly limitless choices, turns out to be our response to a Jewish voice that speaks from deep within us. Our homecoming is also a return to Sinai.

THE THREE FESTIVALS:
SINAI AND THE SACRED CYCLE

As Creation is celebrated by Shabbat, revelation is celebrated primarily by the cycle of the three annual festivals we call *shalosh regalim,* the three seasons of pilgrimage to Jerusalem. These three represent a cycle, the high point of which is Shavuot, the day that commemorates Sinai itself. The celebration of these festivals, and with them the rhythm of the sacred calendar as a whole, is our way of making the ancient tales of our ancestors' wanderings into vessels through which our own inner tales are told. In them, our own seeking and wandering find meaning.

The cycle begins with Pesach, the festival of liberation. We set out on our path and begin the journey with liberation from Egypt. The freedom we celebrate here is at once collective and individual, national and personal. The Egypt from which we are liberated is that of national oppression and loss of our distinctive Jewish identity. It is also the Egypt of alienation from our root in Y-H-W-H and from the inability both to turn inward to know ourselves and to act to transform our lives. This Egypt is described in our sources both as *galut ha-da'at,* the exile of the mind, and *galut ha-dibbur,* the exile of language. The Hebrew word for Egypt, *Mitsrayim,* is regularly described as derived from *metsar yam,* "the narrow straits of the sea." On these festivals, in the Hallel psalms we thank the One to whom "I called from the narrow straits" and who "answered me in the breadth of YaH." Liberation is an opening up of the bonds, a refusal to be dominated any longer by the interests of our narrowest self. It is a seeing beyond ego and its constant demands, an opening to "the breadth of YaH," the vision of God in Creation.

Mind and word are both in bondage. The series of events that leads to Sinai begins in Egypt; the word cannot be spoken within us until the mind is freed from its own constrictions. But the link between Egypt and Sinai is crucial on other levels as well. Sinai is an act of covenant and commitment, the marriage of God and Israel. We are not able to make such a commitment until we are free, until we are whole enough to turn fully to the other. The fact that Sinai is preceded by liberation from Egypt forces us to recognize that, for others as well as ourselves, liberation takes precedence to commitment. The struggle to be free in all of its many forms (including freedom from religion itself when it becomes a source of bondage), is a sacred struggle. Our calendar connects these two events, the liberation from bondage and the standing before Sinai, in a special way. Beginning with the day after the Exodus, we count fifty days, the period of the Omer, in anticipation of Shavu'ot, the anniversary of Sinai.

Revelation depends on freedom. The covenant of Sinai could only be made by a free people. True commitment to life in the presence of Y-H-W-H, for the individual as well, must begin with freedom. The miracle that sets the whole process of these great events in motion, according to one hasidic view, takes place neither on Pesach nor on Shavu'ot, but rather earlier, on the tenth of Nisan. That was the day on which the Israelites in Egypt set aside lambs for the offering in anticipation of the Exodus. On that day, they decided they could no longer live in slavery. They defied their Egyptian masters by preparing to celebrate their liberation, an act from which there was no turning back. This statement of defiance, the realization that there is no life without freedom, is the real miracle, to which all the "signs and wonders" of Egypt are merely commentary.

But liberation is not only a prelude to Sinai. We have had occasion earlier to mention that the rabbis described two moments as those when all Israel saw the divine Glory: at the splitting of the Sea, and when standing before Mount Sinai. To describe the splitting of the Sea as a moment of revelation on its own is an important statement. It says that liberation *itself* is a form of revelation. One of the moments when the face of God is revealed to us is the moment when we set ourselves free. The "handmaiden at the sea," who saw more than the greatest prophets, had her vision in the moment when she knew she was free. The sacred exhilaration of that moment should not be lost on us. It was human courage (Nachshon walking into the Sea) that brought forth the vision of God's presence. Sometimes we rush too quickly to link Pesach and Shavu'ot, as though to say that Pesach itself is incomplete, that it is a mere prelude to revelation. Here let it be said that we know of a revelation that happens in the moment when humans are set free, as we know of one when they proclaim God's unity and declare themselves to be part of the great One. Each of these sacred moments, in order to be whole, needs completion by the other.

Pesach is celebrated by the great sacred meal, the seder, at which we tell again to a new generation with song, story, and feasting, the tale of our liberation. Shavu'ot is celebrated by study, spending the whole night awake in enjoyment of To-

rah, anticipating the dawn, when the tale of Sinai is read once
again.

The primary setting for celebration of Pesach is the family.
Each household, the Torah tells us, took as much food from
the sacrifice as its members needed to eat. In our day, where
the community or havurah celebrates Pesach together, it is
taking on the family role. But on Shavu'ot, the primary locus
of celebration is that of community. The community of those
who share Torah together teach and study through the night,
making the text live again for one another. Here, the community embodies that community of old that stood as one before
the mountain.

The cycle that begins with Pesach and reaches its height on
Shavuot is drawn to conclusion on Sukkot, the third of the
pilgrimage festivals. Sukkot may best be described as a celebration of living-in-the-world, a time when the lofty realities
represented by the earlier festivals and by the just-passed
season of *teshuvah,* or return and renewal, are brought into the
ordinariness of daily life. To do this, we forsake the home in a
way and thus transform it. We show that we build our lives,
after all, in the frailest of dwellings. The *sukkah* is a place
where the smallest of blessings is a great joy. Sukkot is the
time when we take nothing more than fruit and branches to
"rejoice before the Lord."

It is striking that the holiday cycle ends with Sukkot, which
historically commemorates the wandering of Israel in the
wilderness. There is no holiday to celebrate our arrival into
the land, the conclusion of the journey. We begin by throwing
off the yoke, we count the days to the moment of covenant
and commitment, then we set off on our wanderings until we
begin again with liberation. There seems to be a message built

into this structure that points to a deeper meaning than that of the history of ancient Israel alone. The journey at which the symbols of the sacred year are pointed is an unending and cyclical one. Its fulfillment, as seen from the viewpoint of revelation, lies not in its conclusion (or in "arrival" at the final goal), but rather in its self-renewing power. While there are various messianic themes associated with Sukkot, its redemptive message lies mostly in the contentment of harvest and in our finding God within this world. Here, the tale with which we opened perhaps has to be modified: note that the wise man is still within the kingdom of lies when he comes before the king. Their encounter may be a simpler or more ordinary one than the one the tale describes. The portrait we draw may not be taken all at once, like the snapping of a camera shutter, but may be drawn line by line, day by day, as we wander through that kingdom.

THE WORD IN OUR DAY

At Sinai, the voice of Moses came to bear the voice of God within it. We who believe that revelation is not a onetime event, but an ongoing process, must, with fear and trembling, with deep humility and "holy audacity," allow our voices too to become bearers of that voice. The sound of Y-H-W-H is "a great voice that never ceased." Today it needs us to be its trumpet.

Vav has drawn forth the point of the *Yod,* bringing Divinity from silence into speech. The many words may indeed be our own, but the single Word nevertheless lives within them. That same *Vav,* we should remember, is also the particle of conjunction: it means "and." Through it, one is joined to the other, soul to Soul, word to Word. But the *Vav* as that which joins one to the other is also that which acclaims Sinai as the moment of *yiḥud,* the union of bridegroom and bride. This mystical marriage between the primal pair, conceived alternatively as God and the Community of Israel, or blessed Holy One and *Shekhinah,* is also the union, according to the kabbalists, of *Vav* and *Heh.* Because *Vav* means "and," it calls for union. As such, it too is incomplete in itself, and seeks after its mate. So too does Judaism as revelation remain but "half a body." Those who are called to Sinai are sent forth from there to do the work of redemption. The gathering at the mountain is itself a form of *tsimtsum,* a concentration of energy that takes place only so that those who hear the Word may go forth to realize it in deed. *Vav* calls out for *Heh:* revelation is the call that sets us on the path in search of a world redeemed.

REDEMPTION

Here we are, wanderers in the kingdom of lies. So long have these lies been our reality that we no longer know who we are. We no longer remember the mission on which we were sent. The portrait is forgotten, as our own divine image is tarnished with falsehood. The soul is lost within us, drowned out by the noise of the world, the loud blaring of our own insecurities and fears, as we go about the business of living. We rush to build false security for ourselves: positions, titles, made-up identities that will keep us from the terror. All of these belong to the kingdom of lies. Insofar as they possess us, we too are of that kingdom. When they are stripped away—or so we fear—we will no longer know who we are, why we are living, or how to go forward from day to day.

Somewhere in the deepest recesses of our inner selves, the candle of ancient memory still glows. Covered by countless layers of hurt and defense, by all the ego-crust formed around our inner edges over decades of rushed and battered living, the candle's light is not to be seen. Faith is the intuition that such a light still burns, that emptiness and vanity are not our final lot, that there is a way to journey forward that will also take us back to the source of our own inner light.

This light is the object of our most ancient memory, one that we are ever seeking the words to recall. Even memory is in need of language; the mind requires a vocabulary by which it can articulate that which the heart already knows. Tradition serves us as a source of such language, a well of words upon which we can draw to bring that memory forth to tell its tale.

The Light of the First Day

In the ancient Jewish language we are speaking here, the inner light is said to reflect the earliest "memory" of the world as well as that of each person. When God said, "Let there be light!" on Creation's first day, we are told, the light that came forth was too bright for God's creatures to bear. With it, a person could see "from one end of the world to the other." Such great light, revealing all the secret places of existence, would not allow for life as we know it. We creatures, human and animal alike, need to hide in order to exist. The light itself was thus set aside, in order that we might be able to hide. Only "in the future that is coming" will such hiding no longer be needed. The light of the first day will be brought forth for all to see. In walking toward that future, we reclaim our ancient light.

But where is that light in our own times? Is there some way we can find it without waiting for the very end? The light is said to be hidden in Torah, in the human soul, and in sparks of light that fill and animate the entire world. We are gatherers of light; our task is to bring the sparks together and to reveal this world as a place of light. But we are not allowed to gather them too quickly.

Here again, we are faced with the painful paradox of our human situation. The light is hidden in order that we might exist. The "light of the first day" is the holy lamp that would show us clearly that all is One, that nothing but the One exists, that all of reality is a single whole. But such insight is not given to us mortals except in rare moments—and with good reason! How could we go on with the small tasks that make up our lives, fulfilling our essential role of bringing forth, sustaining, and educating new generations of human beings, if we had such full awareness? If humanity is to exist and to remain human, the light must remain hidden.

But that same humanity desperately needs the light. We cry out for guidance, for some sense that we are walking in the right direction. Human life is impossible without hope, and hope requires that something of the light be revealed. How do we call upon the light to guide us, to lead us in our own search for the truth that it bears within it? The hiding of the primal light, necessary as it might be for our very existence, at the same time appears to us as cruelty, a needless inflicting of pain upon this human creature condemned to seek for meaning.

CRYING OUT FOR THE LIGHT

To that same One who is the source of our hope, the glimmer of light beyond the darkness, we protest the pain of living. We cry out in our hurt and our anger. We understand the need for the light's hiding, and yet we protest it. Surely there is no need for as much darkness as we have known! We have to experience emptiness in order to stretch and grow in spirit. We need to know the absence of light in order to strive forward in our human struggle. But could we not learn these without the deaths of a million children? Could the path to understanding not be strewn with fewer victims, fewer human lives destroyed and abandoned of hope along the way? Every one of those human beings is an image of Y-H-W-H! Each time one of them gives up on life, the divine light grows dimmer. If we care about the diminishing of God's image in our world, we have to cry out.

True encounter with oneness is given to us only in fleeting moments, glimpses quickly forgotten, as we rush onward with our daily lives. In their absence—that seems to us as "the absence of God" or the "hiding of God's face"—religious life becomes an act of defiance. Our faith becomes a rejection of absurdity, a refusal to accept emptiness as our final lot in life. Faith is our testimony—all evidence to the contrary notwithstanding—that the light still burns, that meaning is still to be found. We do not *deny* the absurdity of life. No human being, and especially no Jew, living in the latter half of the twentieth century could do that. We have seen the arbitrariness of fate, the depths of human cruelty, the indifference of both man and nature. We do not deny absurdity, but we reject it, we *defy* it. We stare into the face of darkness and proclaim that light still exists. We refuse to give in to hopelessness. The struggle for faith and the refusal to give in to despair are one and the same.

Confronting reality as fully as anyone who lives in our world, we know that there is another side to reality as well. The absence of God and the rule of darkness certainly represent a truth, one we do not deny. But we know a deeper truth as well. Here we are sustained by memory. The glow of those moments in which we glimpsed God's light still warms us. We Jews know, and sometimes still feel, the warmth of that glow from Sinai. The fire of God's mountain still burns, we proclaim, encircling and warming those who study Torah. But really that light burns in every person, the memory of those moments in our lives that were closest to true freedom, to understanding, and thus to fulfillment. These are "the Sea" and "Sinai" in our individual lives, the moments that inspire us and keep us on course in our journey.

The light within us needs to be rekindled, needs to have its glow restored. This usually comes about when we see a glimpse of that same light shining in another. That other may be a *tsaddik*—a righteous one whose light shines with a special brightness—or perhaps just an ordinary person, like the one who reminded Nahman Kossover of the face of God. There are moments when we can catch that glow in the most ordinary of people, usually in moments of giving, caring, or somehow showing a generosity of spirit that opens their light to our view. At such a time, that person sheds ordinariness and becomes for us a momentary *tsaddik*. The light we see in that moment is that of Y-H-W-H, the One beyond all form. The same Being beyond names, or unspeakable Word beyond and within all words, is also the eternal source of inner light. As the One calls us into being, so does it cry out from within us to seek out its light in others, to brighten the light that glows within ourselves, and to draw others to that light. Our sharing of the light is the beginning of our homeward journey.

Redemption as Coming Home

We are coming home. The journey is almost complete. "The King has brought me into His chambers." The fourth letter of the divine name represents *Shekhinah,* divine presence as it dwells in matter, the sparks of holy light scattered throughout the world. This final letter of God's name has been separated from the three that precede it, wandering through an eternity of exile, just as we have been wanderers in that great and painful chasm that lies between revelation and redemption, between our first glimmer of Y-H-W-H and our ability to transform the world in the light of that vision. Our return home is the return of Holy One and *Shekhinah* to one another, the reunion of cosmic male and female, cosmic parent and cosmic child. It is also the rejoining of Y-H-W-H within to Y-H-W-H beyond, the reunion of Being-in-all-its-forms with *Eyn Sof,* the changeless One. Here, we proclaim that "beyond" and "within" are one, that the great unity is one with all and with each of its wandering sparks.

Home is Y-H-W-H, the beginning and the end of our journey. The One who has sent us forth on our way and the One we discover at the end of all our wanderings are truly one and the same. Only as we come home do we understand that every step of the journey had its special place and meaning, that our particular face of the One had to be encountered in just this way and no other.

Home is earth, the mother we abandoned so very many centuries ago. Homecoming is our return to our source within this world, to the great womb out of whom we are ever being born, the one to whom we ever return. Homecoming is the rejoining of matter and spirit, an understanding that this most primal of all separations stands as the cause of our alienation from ourselves, from the deepest roots of our own tradition, and from the very earth that nurtures us. Our return is the great act of healing, one directed toward all of these at once: we must heal ourselves, for we are fragmented; we must heal our tradition, for it has been distorted, leading us to less than a full embrace of the One; we must heal the earth, restoring to her that which generations have plundered, while there is yet time. The hour is late. Our homecoming takes place not a minute too soon.

Home is Jerusalem, the place to which we all return: heavenly Jerusalem and earthly Jerusalem, now revealed to be one and the same. There is only one city, the one at the center of all the worlds. This Jerusalem is the heart of the world, the center of life, and the font of its renewal. She is the hill to whom all turn in awe; she is the whole one from whom all wholeness flows. "For My house shall be called a House of Prayer for All Peoples." Everyone will turn toward this center, though each of those peoples may call it by a different name.

Home is the Land of Israel, and the homecomer is the Jewish people, survivor of the world's longest exile. We will return to our land, learn to live with our brother/our enemy, and reconnect our future with our most ancient past. The return of Jews to Y-H-W-H through the language of our tradition, and the return of Jews to the land of our birth, are both, in ways that we do not yet comprehend, a part of the same return. The return of Israel is one of the great mysteries of our age.

Home is the human heart. Our return to Y-H-W-H is in no way separate from our return to ourselves, to the point of inward truth out of which our humanity shines forth. "Return to Me and I shall return to you." The return is always mutual, always that of two lovers returning to their single heart. As we come home to ourselves, *Shekhinah* within us is joined to her source, and the new light that radiates from the source embraces and warms us as well. "The Compassionate One desires the heart." There is no return except the return to our heart.

Home is male and female, the restored harmony of man and woman. Surely, a part of the journey homeward is the reunion of those inner polarities we designate as "male" and "female," an integration of the self in which the qualities associated with the two genders are brought into balance with one another. There is no wholeness for us humans that leaves aside this most basic of human dualities. As we come home to ourselves, each of us will have learned along the way to accept the sexual "other" that lies hidden inside us. This integration will allow for a new acceptance by men and women of one another, as well as an acceptance by all of us of the complex intertwining of male and female that lies within. As it will make for greater and less tortured self-love, so will it allow for fuller, more joyous, and less threatened expression of all our love for one another.

Home is Eden, the place we fled so long ago. Eden represents innocence, a place where we are most fully at home with ourselves. It is the world as it was before exile came to be. For those who are still in Eden, there is no distance from home, no expulsion from the place of light, none of that exile from self that we call alienation. But Eden has been lost to us since childhood, or perhaps has existed for us only in our adult fantasy of what childhood should have been. We return to that ideal child within us, to the place of perfection that only the child can know.

The Bible: A Tale of Exile

The Bible begins its account of human history with a tale of exile and wandering. Our first parents are exiled from the Garden for the crime of separating knowledge from life, for eating of the one tree without the other. This very first act of separation cut off the special human ability to know or comprehend from its own root in affirmation and celebration. Knowledge and life became two trees, rather than one. *Da'at* or "knowing," with its overtones of intimacy and union, became pursuit of knowledge, an act of the intellect alone. Hence the genesis of disembodied mind, a primal violation of the state of nature, one that falsely separates this "knowing" from "knowledge," gathered up by the mind alone. Because of this first separation, the Tree of Knowledge was led into its own inner moral duality, having to divide between "good" and "evil." The possibility that human knowledge could be used to destroy life—realized on such an awful scale in our own century—is the ultimate perversion of human existence as seen from the perspective of Eden.

If this is the sin that took us out of Eden, what is its redemption? How do we restore to the human soul the wholeness that binds together and unifies knowledge and life? Our answer to this question lies in the life of Torah, our Tree of Life. We commit ourselves to a different sort of learning, one that has all the vitality and urgency of our commitment to life itself. We learn Torah not as intellectual exercise, not out of historical curiosity, but because it is our vehicle for expressing the deep yearnings of our souls. *Into the hands of Torah, shaped so lovingly by our ancestors over many generations, we place our souls.* In telling the tales of the exodus and the wandering, in recounting the details of how our first God-dwelling was made, even in bemoaning the role of women in the Torah or in screaming out its wrongness in the murderous prescription for the Canaanites, we are telling *our* story. We set our own lives, our own quest, into the ever-renewed framework of ancient Torah. Out of Torah we derive *ḥukkey ḥayyim,* rules and boundaries that make for life. The language of Torah becomes a symbolic path we come to follow on our own journeys. Our stake in Torah, both as a people and as individuals, is a vital one. This way of knowledge becomes a tree of life for us, rebinding us to the tree from which we turned aside so long ago.

The knowledge gained by our first parents—the earliest humans—allowed them to view themselves as separate from the rest of the natural order. True, they had been created "on the same day" as the beasts; humanity in many ways remains a part of the animal kingdom. But their creation had a special character. They alone were said (by themselves, of course) to be "in the image" of their Creator. They distorted this sense of "image" to have it mean that they could do whatever they liked in the Garden, as though they were its rulers. They discovered quickly that it was in their hands to trample and destroy the Garden, more easily than to "work it and guard it." Then the Garden had to be protected against this dangerous and arbitrary human force of will. The sword was there—set in place by the fiery angel of human conscience—to keep us out, lest we do harm.

Driven by God—or by our own inner demons—from our

first home, Adam and Eve's children became wanderers. The punishment of exile, "wandering and wavering shall you be in the earth," describes the universal human situation since the time of Cain. These most basic facts of adult existence, alienation and the longing for home, are taken by our tradition to reflect the most dire of punishments. It is this sense of exile and homelessness that connects the historical experience of the Jewish people with the most universal suffering of humanity.

The placement of this tale of exile at the Bible's opening has to be seen as prophetic when viewed in the light of Jewish history. This people, whose central experience for nearly two millennia was to be that of homelessness, early in its history posited exile as the greatest of human sufferings. It is this ongoing pain of exile in which we Jews say that God takes part. The divine presence goes into exile, sharing in the pain of Israel and humanity. "Every place where Israel were exiled, *Shekhinah* was exiled with them." The exile of Israel from its holy land, the place of its origin and the site of its promised redemption, is thus uplifted and transformed into a dramatic replay, on the grand scale of history, of the human condition. *We Jews are a parable of the human situation,* both in our exile and in our faithfulness. Wherever men and women are exiled, the divine presence is there with them, suffering in their pain at the loss of home, sharing in their dreams of return and redemption.

The generations of Adam's children, in the biblical tale, live out their exile from paradise without finding a way to maintain or protect God's image in an unprotected world. Murder, idolatry, violent debauchery, false attempts to reach heaven, all mark the vanity of life in those early generations.

Having nearly despaired of humanity as a whole and its fate, the Bible then turns to the tale of a single family, that of Abraham and Sarah and their offspring. The hope is that somehow they and their tribe will be able to recreate what was lost in Eden. Indeed, we first meet Abraham as he is told by God to leave his home and seek out a new land, one that is to be described later as "flowing with milk and honey," or in various other terms that were to remind us of Eden. This land is to serve as home for Abraham's family, as the site of his worship, and as the object of God's promise to his descendents.

It is these descendents who become the chief object of Abraham's concern. He and Sarah enter the land as an aging and childless couple, unimpressed by the various blessings God offers, unless there are to be future generations to inherit them. The divine voice within this barren, would-be parent cries out that he will be father of so many that they will be compared to the stars of heaven, or to the grains of sand at the sea. His faith in following this voice marks the first step in the path we still seek to walk. His and his beloved Sarah's longing for children shapes for all time the Jewish concern for off-spring, and our devotion to passing down our tradition from one generation to another. To break that link between gener-ations is to break faith with this wonderful old couple who put so much trust in us, the descendents for whom they prayed. No wonder that even Jews who live far from Torah still shudder at the thought of not teaching it and passing it on to their children and grandchildren.

Over the course of the next three generations, Abraham and his children wander in and out of the land, never quite fully taking root in it. Famine sends them to Egypt or to the Philistine cities on the coast; marriage roots take them back to their old Mesopotamian homeland. Finally, in the fourth generation, the elusive new home slips away from them altogether, as Jacob and his family become settled—and then enslaved—in Egypt.

Thus far the Book of Genesis serves as a prologue to the rest of Torah, indeed to all of Jewish history. From Exodus onward, Israel's task is that of homecoming, of restoring and enhancing that bit of wholeness it had while living in its own most holy place, its own new Eden. *Torah is the tale of our search for home.*

We come forth from Egypt, needing first to be free if our journey homeward is to begin at all. Once free, we meet Y-H-W-H in the wilderness and take into ourselves that commitment to know the divine life that lives in all of being. In the light of Sinai we build the community and develop the path that will guide us when we enter the land. We wander and struggle, falling prey to temptation and faithlessness, learning the cruel lessons that will be needed in the fashioning of a people. But our Torah ends just before the return to homeland is achieved. We stand with Moses, having wandered through the desert, looking across the Jordan, ready to enter the promised land. But then Moses dies, the world is created all over again, and the story begins once more.

This is the pattern of Jewish life as lived for countless generations, the life of the synagogue as it has been passed down to us. It is an endless cycle, an endless exercise of preparation, from one point of view, for that final act of crossing the river, a step that is never taken. In our generation, the Jewish people has taken that step toward its own redemption, one that makes our era different from all that have come before.

Finally, we will all come home,—humans to Eden, Jews to the Land of Israel, women and men to one another, parents and children—joyously bearing the dreams that have sustained us, dreams tied like bundles of sheaves across our backs. The dream of Israel is that of old Jerusalem made new, purified of hatred and conflict, open to all. "The mountain of Y-H-W-H's house established over all the mountains . . ." "My house will be a house of prayer for all people"—our own Jewish vision, to be sure, but one we have come to accept in its most universalist sense. *To understand us Jews is to realize that we are eternal servants of that vision, even priests at its altar.*

Homecoming and *Teshuvah*

Coming home is *teshuvah,* but in the fullest sense of that rich term. This word for "turning" or "returning" means much more than "repentance," as it is often translated. *Teshuvah* is the universal process of return. All things turn toward their center, as fully and as naturally as plants grow in the direction of light, as roots reach toward their source of water. The same universal will that is manifest in the evolution of life, ever striving toward "higher" forms of consciousness, is present in the desire of all things to turn inward and to show that they are tied to their single source. The world that flows forth from the One seeks to return to the One. Y-H-W-H is manifest throughout being, we recall, only to attest anew in each moment to the oneness of all that is. Each individual being contains within it the presence of all being, the fullness of Y-H-W-H. From the moment that "separate" reality exists, its heart is filled with a longing to recreate the primal state of oneness, to be reunited with the source of all life.

This universal longing is marked in human consciousness by the desire to "return" to God. The human act of contrition that we call *teshuvah* shows this universal tendency as it is manifest in our own lives. We seek to overcome those barriers that keep us from the One, to break down the walls, however thin or even illusory, from one point of view, that separate us from our own truest self. Our desire to return home is the manifestation in the human spirit of the most universal and basic longing, one far more ancient than the individual who feels its pull, or the various cultural forms in which it is seen.

All *teshuvah,* according to the kabbalists, is ultimately *teshuvah* to *binah,* to the first *Heh* of the divine name. This aspect of the Divine represents God as cosmic womb, as great mother of the universe. It is our distance from that ever-nourishing and sustaining root that defines our exile. But it is not only we who are in exile. *Shekhinah* herself, the second *Heh* of Y-H-W-H and mother of the lower worlds, has gone into exile with her children. The one who returns is seen both as Israel, the king's lost son, and as exiled *Shekhinah,* the second *Heh* that is cut off in exile from the other three letters of God's name. She is the lost princess, whose return to the palace is the final redemption. Thus, our dream language of redemption is that of *mother* and *daughter,* as well as that of *father* and *son.* In *teshuvah* we are wayward sons, returning to our royal father; we are also sparks of *Shekhinah*-light, restored to our mother's bosom.

TESHUVAH AND THE SACRED YEAR

Within the cycle of the sacred year, the period devoted to this process is the forty-day cycle culminating in Yom Kippur. Though *teshuvah* takes place each day and in every moment, our annual return begins in the month of Elul, the time called after the verse, "I am my beloved's and my beloved is mine." The season of renewal calls upon us to examine our deeds, to recall our mortality, and to return to the path from which we have inevitably strayed. But ultimately, it points beyond all of these, hinting both at rebirth of the spirit and at a sense of oneness with the Beloved.

The holy days of the Jewish year are both commemoration and reenactment. Our words recall the creation of the world on Shabbat, the liberation from bondage on Pesach, Sinai on Shavu'ot, and so forth. But the inner meaning of these words is a drama of reenactment, in which these great events take place on an inner plane, allowing each Jew to feel him or herself to be a real participant, rather than a distant observer. The promise offered by our tradition that these ways actually work—that something of liberation's light may really be felt by the Jew sitting at the seder table—is attested by the faithfulness of Jews to these ancient forms.

But what is the root of the "days of awe" in the historical drama of ancient Israel? These festivals, at once more personal and more universal than any other in the calendar, are not ordinarily connected with sacred history. There is no apparent event in the biblical narrative that links up with this season.

The rabbis attended to this lack, as they did in the case of Shavu'ot. A connection unmentioned in Scripture is offered in the *aggadah*. The rabbis claim that the New Moon of Elul was the date when Moses went up the mountain to receive the second tablets. He returned with them, having achieved the forgiveness of Israel, forty days later, on Yom Kippur.

The holiest day on our calendar is, then, the commemoration of an event nearly forgotten. It is a second holiday of revelation, the day of the giving of the second tablets. This is the occasion when Moses cries out to see God's glory, and is hidden in the cleft of Sinai's rock as the glory passes by. In that moment, God's thirteen attributes of mercy are called out (again "in the voice of Moses"?). The recitation of these becomes a verbal talisman of atonement, and their frequent repetition forms the core of our penitential liturgy (*selihot*), throughout this season, and especially on Yom Kippur. It is presumably a year later, and in commemoration of this event, that the great atonement ritual of the tabernacle is enacted, the model for our Yom Kippur.

Why should the giving of the second tablets have this central role? Why should a day that our tradition surely considers its calendar's "holy of holies" represent a mere repetition, the giving again of that which had already been accepted and received on Shavu'ot? Perhaps it is because the second tablets represent a *renegotiated marriage* between God and the Jewish people, and this is what Yom Kippur is all about. The first tablets, given on Shavu'ot, were fashioned entirely by God: "The tablets were of God's workmanship and the writing was God's writing." Israel was overwhelmed by all this divinity and the radical transformation it demanded; hence our flight to the golden calf. We mere humans could not live with the intensity of demand implied by such a Torah. God's Torah called upon us to be godlike to a degree we could not stand. We had to seek out an idol, divinity in a form of our own making.

By the time of the second tablets, God had learned a lesson about dealing with these human creatures. "Carve yourself two tablets of stone like the first ones," God says to Moses on the mountain, "and I will write upon them." This new marriage is to be a partnership, fashioned together of human and divine effort. Moses does the carving, God does the writing. This marriage seems to have lasted significantly longer than the first.

This is the message of our "days of awe." There is a possibility of return, of coming home. The original harmony—be it that of parent and child, or of a young and improperly balanced marriage—may have ended in pain and separation. But there is a way to come back. With real human participation in the terms of reunion, the way home remains open, and the prospects for longevity of relationship—if they are to be judged by Jewish history—are more than good. In this lies the eternal optimism of Jewish faith. It is expressed for us in the verse, "As You have borne this people from Egypt up to here," which introduces the thirteen qualities of mercy. However far we think we have to go in life, however distant we feel from the goal, we need only recall where we were when we started. Our faith in the One has brought us from Egyptian bondage to the place where we are now. Surely that same faith, if it has brought us all this distance, can carry us the rest of the way as well!

This dream of restored wholeness is sounded out dramatically by the shofar blasts, the central symbolic expression of the *teshuvah* season. The shofar sound represents prayer beyond words, an intensity of longing that can only be articulated in a wordless shout. But the order of the sounds, according to one old interpretation, contains the message in quite explicit terms. Each series of shofar blasts begins with *teki'ah,* a whole sound. It is followed by *shevarim,* a tripartite broken sound whose very name means "breakings." "I started off whole," the shofar speech says, "and I became broken." Then follows *teru'ah,* a staccato series of blast fragments, saying: "I was entirely smashed to pieces." But each series has to end with a new *teki'ah,* promising wholeness once more. The shofar cries out a hundred times on Rosh Hashanah: "I was whole, I was broken, even smashed to bits, but I shall be whole again!"

But our restoration of wholeness is not to be achieved by prayer alone. As indicated earlier, the liturgy only brings us to the edge of the Jordan, but never takes us across into the promised land. For this we need to add the *deed* to our holy thoughts and words. *Teshuvah* and *tefillah* ("prayer") need *tsedakah* ("righteous doing") in order to be effective. We restore the world (and God's name) to wholeness only by doing. In fact, our entire contemplative effort has been pointed toward realization in the realm of action. We are the bearers of compassion in this God-filled universe; so too are we "the limbs of the *Shekhinah,"* the only ones who can make real in this world our vision of wholeness. Redemption is brought about only by the deed.

THE REDEMPTIVE TASK:
GETTING TO WORK

Our commitment to the redeeming deed applies, in the first place, to life within the human community. We take it as our task to enhance each person's potential for realizing the divine image, remembering that each of us bears a portrait unique and vital to the wholeness of Y-H-W-H. But how clear can that portrait be when its bearer is suffering from hunger? Or from political oppression? Or from domestic bondage? Or when the person is hurting self and others, due to a compulsion from which it seems impossible to break free? If we are going to enhance the divine image in this world, we must work to maximalize human freedom, always remembering that it was only after we came out of bondage that we were able to look toward God's mountain. That commitment to freedom also includes helping people to create the sorts of lives and social structures to allow that freedom a lasting and secure home. Our Judaism lives in those two essential moments when we discover God. *We celebrate (and guard) our freedom, knowing Y-H-W-H at the Sea, and we build a community that lives in God's presence, knowing Y-H-W-H at the mountain.* Our role is to share these twin values with others, to help other parts of the human family, each in the way of its own traditions, to achieve both freedom and responsible community.

In our day, the work of redemption applies to the nonhuman world in which we live, as well as to the human community. Our responsibility to the natural order, long neglected in a tradition that focused all too narrowly on "God, Torah, and Israel" (what, then, of *world?*), needs to be restated. This restatement has happened first among Jews living in Israel, as might be expected. There, a new Judaism is being articulated, one that involves *land* and *language* more than it does observance or tradition. Although the balance in those efforts is tilted away from tradition in ways that make us uncomfortable, we have much to learn from them. We Diaspora Jews have remained too much *luftmenschen,* too urbanized and overly intellectualized to take cognizance of divinity in our natural surroundings. This has begun to change in our day, as Jewish names begin to appear among lists of birdwatchers and mountain climbers, as well as those of Talmudists and theoretical physicists. Making the world whole or returning to the One has no meaning unless we do so in the context of living in greater harmony with our natural surroundings and creating a way of life that keeps us at peace with nature's own law.

In placing the deed at the center of religious activity, we seek a Judaism inspired at once by the prophets of Israel and by the mystic teachers of a later age. It was our ancient prophets who first delivered to the world the message that God's true will could only be fulfilled by justice, that divine law referred, in the first sense, to the rescue of those whom society made its victims. This, they taught, is God's great passion, arousing love for those who fulfill it and anger against those who stand in its way. It is moral deed rather than priestly cant that has the power to transform both self and world. The recovery of this moral passion and the need to act upon it is the major achievement of liberal Judaism in modern times.

The deed, as promulgated by the kabbalists, has a rather different sense. Their understanding of the *mitsvot* went farther than that of the prophets. They understood that the cosmos itself is to be saved by human action, that God is in need of a redemption, to be effected through us. *Here, the Divine and the human are joined together: both are redeemer and both are redeemed.* This step is a great help for us who refuse to draw clear lines between God's work and the human task, or between the divine and human realms altogether. The kabbalistic emphasis on the efficacy of the human act is the ultimate denial of nihilistic or cynical views of our role in this world. It is nothing less than *the saving of God* with which each and every person is charged.

For the kabbalists of old, this role was limited to Jews, and especially to those initiated in the secret lore. The deeds that bore this redemptive power were the *mitsvot,* commanded by God's own word, especially such ritual-mysterious acts as the donning of tefillin, blowing the shofar, or waving the lulav. Our *mitsvot* include these, to be sure, and we remain in awe of the profound power they have to enrich our inner lives. But the center of religious obligation for us lies in the realm of *beyn adam le-ḥavero,* the realization of divinity through deeds within the human community. These remain *mitsvot* for us, obligations created and acknowledged in the course of creating a Jewish community, and forms of service that respond to the all-embracing divine word. Such deeds, we claim, have the power to reunify the divine name—or to redeem Y-H-W-H.

We receive the legacies of both prophet and mystic in the spirit of religious humanism. We recognize that our human limbs are the only limbs that exist in this world to bear upon them the truly divine gift of compassion. It is with no particular sense of triumph that we acknowledge this. Nor do we allow ourselves to become "secularized" by this realization, made ready to plunge headlong into the doing of worldly good—or worldly evil—while casting off the sacred like an old, unwanted cloak. Religious humanism, as I understand it, means a realization that the task is ours to do; we no longer wait for the divine hand, separate from our own, to come and save. But this acceptance of responsibility is itself a sacred act for us. We seek to accept, with deeply humbling gratitude, the role of actor for divine compassion in the world of physical reality. The voice of God *does* speak to us at Sinai, but it is none other than the voice of Moses. The hands and feet of God *do* bring redemption, but they are none other than our own limbs, offered by us to our Maker in order to fulfill their true purpose.

Rebalancing the Three Pillars

Though our activist commitment is, by nature, directed outward, we recognize the continuing need for spiritual nurturance of the active life. A rich life of both study and prayer provides the grounding and inner resource so needed by those who endlessly give and serve. We need to restore the balance of Torah, worship, and acts of compassion, proclaimed by our ancient sages as the three pillars on which the world exists. Modern Jewish life has seen an unfortunate "division of labor" in the collective efforts of Jewry. Jews most concerned with acts of compassion, especially those who extend these most universally, are often cut off entirely from both study and worship in a Jewish context. Weak roots bode ill for the ongoing success of their efforts, or for their ability to withstand the inevitable pressures and disappointments of such a life. Others in our community are devoted wholly to proper worship, to the punctilious observance of the commandments, so much so that compassion itself can sometimes be forgotten as a value, especially when it comes to extending that compassion to those outside the community of observant Jews. Torah study in the modern Jewish world (with the notable exception of Orthodoxy) has gone into exile, wandering from the Jewish House of Study to the university department of religion or Judaic Studies. Study has become the realm of academics, from whom it seems appropriate to have no special expectations in the other two realms. From a Jewish point of view, there is something deeply

disturbing about this separation; it is a rift we need to heal. We
need Jews who embody all three of these values, drawing
them together by the example of their lives.

We differ from our mystical forbears in that we no longer
assert that the task of redemption is to be effected by Jews
alone. Our language of homecoming, *teshuvah,* and redemption is the vehicle through which we realize the presence of
Y-H-W-H in this world. But humanity has many such languages, and we have every reason to believe that the divine
presence is contained in those vehicles, as well as in ours. We
cannot know God as manifest in other such sacred languages,
because we are fully given to our own. To speak any such
language requires the whole of the human self; thus any
individual can, under ordinary circumstances, speak but one
of them. But we know with all our heart that Y-H-W-H is
One, and that all humans are bearers of God's presence. It is
inconceivable that the One would not manifest itself
throughout the variety of human cultures and religious expressions, much as it is manifest in the infinite varieties of
natural phenomena. For this richness and variety of spiritual
life among the peoples of this world, we find ourselves
praising God.

Redemption
and the Messianic Dream

T his vision of return and all the dreams that accompany it are the content of our messianic faith. They are embodied for us in the figure of messiah, the Jewish symbol for the redemption of this world. Messiah represents the fulfillment of human history, the final assertion that our shared journey, after all, has been toward a goal. We refer to that goal as *le-takken olam bemalkhut Shaddai,* "to establish this world as God's kingdom." The vision includes the perfection of God's creation in a transformed and purified natural order. Lions will lie down with lambs and nations will make war no more: the natural and historic orders will be transformed together as the gulf between humanity and nature disappears in "God's kingdom." This is the faith of *Barukh Shem;* we look forward to a world in which each creature and every moment will indeed attest to the oneness of Y-H-W-H. In this messianic faith are embodied countless generations of Jewish hope, the refusal of Jews to give in to oppression and despair, our collective dream that this very imperfect world could yet be the site of divine redemption in all its glory.

The messianic dreams and fantasies of Jews, rooted in the ancient longing for restored Davidic kingship, grew at a fast pace in the periods when Jews lived under persecution, first, that of Romans and Persians, later, that of Christendom and Islam. Every great conquest or revolutionary movement

brought forth renewed messianic dreams, each of these
building on top of all the other fantasies that had come before.
In the canon of Jewish tradition, the sources that record these
dreams stand at the polar opposite from the realm of law: they
are entirely without system or order, unconfined by the
dreary limitations of reality, completely nonbinding on the
reader—but highly attractive in their own fantastic ardor.

We are heirs to a chaos of messianic dreams, piled up in the
attic of our collective memory in no particular order at all.
Jumbled together in a hopeless confusion, they defy us to sort
them out. Will messiah come to a single generation? Why,
then, should that generation be privileged above all others?
And will that generation die, or live right on into eternity?
Where are the dead until messiah comes? In the Garden of
Eden? Why, then, do they need redemption? And how about
the resurrection? How will there be room for everybody in
the world at the same time? And what about widows and
widowers who remarry? Who will take care of all the fights?
And how about transmigration? In which of its several bodies
will the wandering soul appear? How about the glories of
nature in messianic times? Will people really no longer have to
plant in order to reap bounty? Will we live in this world or in
the heavens? Is the messianic banquet a onetime event, or does
it go on forever? Who will lead the *benschen,* and will they still
sing it to that awful tune? And what happens afterward? After
messiah, if there is an "after?" And after the resurrection?
After the world is made perfect in God's kingdom? What
happens *after* all that?

These questions, and hundreds more like them fill our
fantasy minds, as the child within us hears messianic tales and
tries to imagine "what it will be like." But the central feature

of these tales seems to be their jumbled character. The very looseness of this heritage seems to tell us to take it lightly, as a goad to our own imagination, rather than as burdensome, literal truth.

The figure of messiah remains our symbol of hopes and dreams still not abandoned, needed more than ever in a world that can see the face of its own destruction. But our vision of human perfectibility no longer culminates in a single human being, any more than our sense of origins really goes back to the primal pair in Eden. We see the evolution of our species continuing to move forward, however haltingly, toward the existence of humans who have ever greater depths of awareness or consciousness of divinity than we think possible. We see a human race, some thousands of years in the future, that looks upon us as one of the ancient empires, advanced for its day in technological matters, but rather primitive in its understanding of the universe, and quite awfully childish in its moral conduct. We see that later age dwarfed by still another, and yet another, beyond that. Somewhere in that ongoing growth of understanding and compassion, we glimpse messiah, the human self most fully open to the One, perhaps the human self that stands at the very far edge of transcending what we understand as "human" altogether, reaching out to a presently unknown new world. Such fulfilled humanity will be that which is most fully aware of its role in joining together what we ancients would have called "beyond" and "within," realizing and proclaiming the oneness of all being.

MESSIAH: ACTOR OR HERALD?

We modern Jews have meanwhile rebelled against messiah, or at least against the idea of eternal waiting. We see redemption too much as process to allow ourselves to sit by and pray for the advent of the one who will make it happen. We rather seek out the spark of messianic soul within ourselves, trying to set ourselves to work at some part of messiah's task. Messianic faith is made real for us not by endless generations of patient waiting, but by doing the work of redemption day after day. As to the ultimate usefulness of all these labors and their place in the great scheme of things—generally we prefer not to ask.

The fact is that this rebellion against *waiting* as the chief value of messianic faith took place even before the modern era. It was among the mystical dreamers who lived prior to modernity that Jewish messianism was transformed from a passive faith to a realm of participatory action. Kabbalists believe, as we have said, in the cosmic efficacy of the commandments. Observance, they claim, is not only testimony to Israel's love of God and faith in Sinai, as other pious Jews would say, but is to be seen as an active engagement in the drama of redemption. While the mystics practice the same Judaism as others, the focus of their faith is the process of redemption, rather than the dutiful and patient fulfillment of divine law.

This vision is tied to the kabbalistic myth of Creation, to which we have already referred several times. Before Creation, we will recall, Y-H-W-H was all-in-all; the non-God did not exist in any sense. The One was indeed *Eyn Sof,* without limit or end. When the desire arose within that One to create a realm of otherness (or, in our language, "when" the One put on the garments of the many), its first act had to be one of self-contraction, creating a void within which the non-God, or the relative non-God, might exist. This contraction, or *tsimtsum,* creating the void, resulted also in a concentration of divine energy, poised at the point of a creative leap outward. A beam of divine energy was then sent forth into the void, bearing within it the seeds of all future being. The void, however, emptied of divinity as it was, could not bear the intensity with which this new infusion of energy came at it. Emptiness and fullness were too much polar opposites to exist in harmony. As a result, the "vessels" containing this light or energy were smashed and scattered, somewhat like a fine glass beaker filled with hot liquid would shatter if cast suddenly into extreme cold.

The world originates in this cosmic cataclysm. Our universe is a "broken" one, even before it comes to be. The breakage is reconfirmed, according to most kabbalists, but not initiated, by the sin of Adam and Eve, who then set human history on a course that conforms to the broken cosmic order. Since creation—and especially since the emergence of the people Israel—the task is one of *tikkun,* or repairing and setting right the damage that has been done. The kabbalists understand Torah as a cosmic repair-kit guide, helping to locate the sparks of light and shards of broken vessels that lie hidden throughout creation, waiting to be redeemed and uplifted to the One by the conscious devotion of Israel.

This vision of the religious life as the constant gathering of sparks (and conquest of demonic "shells") is one that places all

Israel, but especially the kabbalists themselves, at the center of the redemptive drama. They are daily engaged in the work of *tikkun*, repair of the world, or in *binyan komat ha-Shekhinah*, the upbuilding of *Shekhinah*'s form. It is primarily *Shekhinah*, the "lowest" of the kabbalistic rungs, that is the object of this breakage. It is her form that is broken or unwhole, and she must be restored to wholeness before the union within divinity can take place. The collective efforts of Israel "rebuild" *Shekhinah*, making her once again the perfect bride, about to enter her marriage chamber. *Shekhinah*, or the indwelling aspect of the divine self, is also the final letter *Heh* of the holy name Y-H-W-H. It is *Vav* and *Heh* that have been separated from one another in the "breakage" that resulted in this world. Our task is to restore their union and thus to make the name complete. Restoring the sparks to their source, rejoining *Shekhinah* to her spouse, and uplifting the final *Heh* to God's name are all alternative metaphoric descriptions for the same ongoing task.

But what then of messiah? If all Israel are ever engaged in the work of redemption, who and why is the redeemer? Here, the kabbalists represent a key turning point within the history of Judaism. They understand that messiah comes only at the end point of redemption, rather than at its beginning. Instead of bringing about the onset of redemption, messiah will herald its completion. The actual work of redeeming the world is turned to us in history, and is done by all of us, day by day. Messiah has been waiting in the wings, as it were, since the very beginning of history, ready to come forth when the time is right. According to one legend, he sits among the lepers at the gates of Rome—today we would be likely to find him in an AIDS hospice—tending to their wounds. Only when redemption is about to be completed will messiah be allowed to arrive. *Rather than messiah redeeming us, we redeem messiah.*

This vision of the universe has much to recommend itself to us as a basis for our contemporary self-understanding. Of course we would universalize it, seeing all of humanity, and not just Israel, as working at redemption. We understand that what for us is "the form of the *Shekhinah*," may be "the body of Christ" for Christians, and may have myriad other names as well. For us the separation of *Vav* and *Heh* is the seeming distance between the two sides of Y-H-W-H, the One never divided and the One manifest throughout being. Our redemptive work needs to maintain its focus on bringing these together. The acts by which we choose to effect redemption, as I have already indicated, will have an interpersonal and communal focus, alongside the ritual aspect that is so emphasized in kabbalah. But the admission that we live in a broken universe, that all of human activity is geared toward its healing, and that redemption is the collective effort of all generations—these insights are as contemporary today as they were in Safed four hundred years ago.

SEEKING OUT OUR SPARKS OF LIGHT

Like our ancestors, we, too, are in search of sparks of light. We, too, find them scattered throughout the world, perhaps even in some places where the kabbalists of old would not have dared to look for them. We, too, are guided by Torah in our search, though for us this guidance is more that of the collective ancient wisdom of Divinity as manifest in our people than it is the once-given manual or road map. We search for the sparks by a two-step process that eternally repeats the primal act of *tsimtsum*. We start by turning inward, seeking to gain a vision both of ourselves and of the world around us. We train our inner eye to see the One that underlies the many, to see all of life as the garbing of Y-H-W-H, the single Self. With the renewed concentration of energy that comes from this meditative turn inward, we send ourselves forth into the outer world, there to do the redemptive deed that joins our inward *kavvanah* to reality.

In the course of this search, we come to understand an insight of the early hasidic masters, heirs to the tale of the vessels and the sparks, that had reached them from a prior era. No one can uplift *all* the sparks, they taught. Each of us has a particular root-of-soul, a distinctive spiritual physiognomy, that is entirely shared by no other. Each person can only redeem those sparks that are fit to his or her own soul. Each of us is a finely tuned receiver, aware of the energy flow only at certain frequencies. These alone are the sparks we can redeem. Some of us can go through life without awareness, contributing nearly nothing to the uplifting of those lights that belong to us. Others, perhaps greater or more enlightened souls, can help us on the path.

The source of light may be so deeply hidden within us that we cannot see it, until we lose the faith that it exists at all. Then another, whose light may be more visible to us than our own, shines forth in such a way that our own light is called out of hiding. This other may be a lover, friend, or teacher; the communication may take the form of mountain, well, or bolt of lightning. In our opening to one another, our two lights meet, casting forth a new light. This light is surely brighter and more widely seen than was the sum of our two faint lights as they had existed before our meeting. And so the light grows. The creation of human community is the redeeming of sparks of holy light.

The sparks are uplifted and form a single great light. The form of the *Shekhinah* is built up and restored to wholeness. The final letter *Heh* is joined to God's name, and the broken word becomes Y-H-W-H once again. Let the abstraction of this language not allow us to forget that the redemptive task is made up of real work in the human community: feeding the hungry, clothing the naked, setting captives free. You will not finish this work, the rabbis remind us, but neither are you free to desist from it. The final wholeness of Y-H-W-H, the union of God and world, is made up of restored fragments, one by one: tortured minds, beaten bodies, broken hearts.

It is the unique sparks each of us redeems that form the portrait we must bring home to the one who sent us on our way. Yes, the king we find at the end of our story is the same one we knew at the beginning. But the portrait we bring home—that could not have existed without our having taken every step and misstep, without our having known every bit of pain, doubt, and renewed faith that we encountered along the way. As that portrait, an endlessly profound composite of the way we have looked throughout our years, and at the same time, the changeless face of Y-H-W-H, is hung in its waiting space along the wall, we pronounce an "Amen" to God's first *kaddish* for the long-awaited child who has come home to the embrace of open arms and godly tears.

We began these reflections as we begin our prayers, claiming that God is one. We spoke of *Sh'ma Yisra'el,* the upper unity, the cosmic One beyond all change, and *Barukh Shem,* the One as manifest in constant change throughout the world. But we conclude, again as do our prayers, with another phrase:

כיום ההוא יהיה ה׳ אחד ושמו אחד

"*On that day* will Y-H-W-H be One and its name one." Only then, as we bring redemption near, will we dare to speak of God's oneness. We are on a journey, a journey of *yiḥud ha-Shem* ("unifying the name"), one that proceeds from *proclaiming* God is one, to *making* God one. We began with a declaration of faith; we end with a commitment to transform reality. Our religious life inhabits the territory that lies between these two, between knowing that all reality is indeed one, and realizing that it is only we who can—and must—make that oneness a reality. This is also the territory between our stepping forth from childhood—or Eden—and the completion of our task. We delight to discover that the territory between these two is a rich and fertile field. We are glad to be its workers.

ENDNOTES

INTRODUCTION

p. xvi

This tale by Rabbi Nahman of Bratslav—The tale as presented here is my own "oral" version, the way it comes out when I tell it after decades of retelling. More precise English renditions of it, as well as commentaries, may be found in my *Tormented Master* (University, AL: University of Alabama Press 1979), pp. 355ff. (the translation there is by Elliot Ginsburg), and Arnold J. Band's rendition of *The Tales* (New York: Paulist Press, 1978), pp. 113ff.

GOD AND THE WAYS OF BEING

p. 5

Sh'ma Yisra'el—Israel's confession of faith in God's oneness is found in Deuteronomy 6:4 and following. Its twice-daily recitation is already taken for granted by the earliest rabbinic sources, presumably based on Deuteronomy 6:7 (cf. *Tosefta Berakhot* 3:1). The privilege of proclaiming God's oneness is the essential gift of Israel and that which gives meaning to its own uniqueness (*Berakhot* 6a). In reciting the *Sh'ma*, Israel reflects that its rung of holiness is higher than that of the angels. The heavenly hosts are permitted to mention God's name only after three words: "Holy, holy, holy" (Isaiah 6:3), whereas Israel can mention it after two (*Hullin* 91b). The association of the *Sh'ma* with death, and especially with martyrdom, is also ancient. Cf. the account of R. Akiva's martyrdom in *Berakhot* 61b and the various discussions of this passage. The Akiva tale is clearly related to that of Jacob's deathbed scene in *Pesaḥim* 56b.

Kavvanah—or inward direction is discussed in connection with the *Sh'ma* in *Berakhot* 13a–b. Recitation of the *Sh'ma* serves as the classic example of *kavvanah* in the rabbinic discussions. For the history of this term, see Hyman Enelow's "Kawwana: the Struggle for Inwardness in Judaism" in *Selected Works of Hyman G. Enelow* (Chicago: Privately published, 1935), vol. 4, pp. 252ff. Unfortunately, Enelow's treatment, which is now quite dated, omitted almost all notice of the all-important kabbalistic and hasidic sources. An especially lovely evocation of *kavvanah* is found in Martin Buber's "The Life of the Hasidim" in his *Hasidism and Modern Man* (New York: Horizon, 1958), pp. 71ff.

p. 6

Higher and lower unity—The association of two types of unity with *Sh'ma* and *Barukh Shem* originates in the *Zohar* (1:18b and freq.). It is central to the most basic mystical text of ḤaBaD Hasidism, the second part of the *Tanya,* designated as the Chapter on Unity and Faith. The usage here is an adaptation of the ḤaBaD text, surely one of the most significant brief mystical treatises in Jewish literature. This text has been translated by the ḤaBaD Hasidim (Brooklyn, NY: Kehot, 1962), English ed. The reader is especially directed to Adin Steinsaltz's commentary to this text, *The Long Shorter Way* (Northvale, NJ: Jason Aronson, 1988). On ḤaBaD mysticism in general, see Rachel Elior, "ḤaBaD: The Contemplative Ascent to God" in *Jewish Spirituality* (henceforth: JS), Vol. 2, ed. A. Green (New York: Crossroad, 1987), and her forthcoming book on the subject, *The Paradoxical Ascent to God: The Kabbalistic Theosophy of Habad Hasidism,* to be published by SUNY Press. As will become clear to the informed reader, the present work is a contemporary response to Jewish faith primarily as it is formulated by the two great mystical teachers of the late eighteenth century who founded the Bratslav and ḤaBaD schools. While I do not live either as a Breslover or a ḤaBaDnik, I recognize gratefully the spiritual influence of both these teachers who selected, distilled, and redirected much of the earlier mystical heritage. I believe that a similar process needs to be undertaken in our day, as timeless mystical insights need to be brought into line with contemporary perspectives, both on Judaism and on the world in which we live. This volume attempts a small contribution toward that effort.

"You are the One until the creation of the world"—From the daily liturgy.

Inner gate, outer gate—The Talmud speaks of the one who has learning but no fear of heaven as one who has been given the inner keys but not the outer ones. "How shall he enter?" it asks (*Shabbat* 31b). I see faith in the transcendent mystery of Y-H-W-H as the "inner key," the key to a gateway one cannot enter except through the garden of immanence. Only by proclaiming—in deed as well as in word—that divinity is real in this world—are we given the privilege of a glimpse "beyond." To rush directly toward the mystery and claim to know it (especially in the form of transcendent person) leads too readily to a superficial and overly conventional-ized form of piety, one that has too many answers and never faces the great question: "How shall I enter?" Real life in the world and in the human community is the only way to God. There is no ap-proach to Revelation other than through Creation.

p. 8

Barukh Shem—is recited silently, following the *Sh'ma*. This re-sponse, which is not biblical, was supposedly called out by the assembled throngs in the Temple following the high priest's reci-tation of the name Y-H-W-H on Yom Kippur (*Yoma* 3:8; 4:1). This use of *Barukh Shem* is still found in the synagogue's re-creation of that event in the avodah service on that day. For other use in the Temple, see *Ta'anit* 16b. Its recitation following the *Sh'ma* seems to have been well-established custom already in the second century. Cf. *Pesaḥim* 56a, where this practice is related to the story about Jacob and his sons, mentioned in the first note to this chapter. Since Moses "omitted" it from the Torah, we respect both Jacob, who said it, and Moses, who omitted it, by saying it in a whisper. But other rabbinic sources (*Devarim Rabbah* 2:31 and 36) indicate that *Barukh Shem* was already spoken at Sinai, either by Moses or by the angels. The latter explains its whisper as fitting to a heavenly doxology, one that is really too holy to be recited aloud on earth. It would seem, however, that the practice predates these explanations. Its presence surely indicates that the recitation of *Sh'ma* was to be seen as an awesome event, bearing with it the power of the priest's once-yearly pronunciation of God's holy name.

p. 9

God who "fills" and "surrounds"—The terms *sovev* and *memale* are of kabbalistic origin. They appear in *Zohar Ra'aya Mehemna*

3:225a and elsewhere in the writings of the anonymous author of *Ra'aya Mehemna* and *Tiqquney Zohar*. From there they were taken into the kabbalah of Moses Cordovero, and thence into ḤaBaD Hasidism, where they play a major role. See *Tanya* 2:7 and Elior, op. cit.

The real meaning behind that phrase is that all is God—This simple three-word pantheistic formulation is studiously avoided throughout Jewish theology, even among writers who are very close to such a point of view. It slips out in Yiddish in a private letter written by one of the early ḤaBaD hasidim. This most interesting document has been translated by Louis Jacobs. See his *Seeker of Unity* (New York: Basic Books, 1966), appendix. On the fears that kept hasidic authors from stating their radical pantheistic or panentheistic views more openly, see my article "Hasidism: Discovery and Retreat" in *The Other Side of God,* ed. P. Berger (Garden City NY: Doubleday, 1981).

p. 12

Our earliest ancestors were diggers of wells—Genesis 26:13ff. The spiritual reading of this passage, taken for granted in hasidic writings, goes back many centuries earlier. Cf. R. Bahya ben Asher, writing in thirteenth-century Barcelona, ad loc, where he refers to "opening the sealed heart." The allegorical reading of the patriarchs' wells, in fact, is found as early as Philo. See his *Questions and Answers on Genesis* 4:191. The wells are described there as representing "education and knowledge," and Philo speaks of "the perfect man" who "has the wells in his soul." For a particularly pungent hasidic reading, see A. J. Heschel, *Kotsk, In Gerangel far Emesdikeyt* (Tel Aviv: Menorah, 1973), p. 81. There, the Philistines, who sealed up the wells that Abraham had dug, are described as imitators of Abraham's piety, so filling it with vacuousness that Isaac has to begin all over again by digging himself a new well. On the notion that Abraham found truth by turning inward, see the sources quoted in my *Devotion and Commandment: The Faith of Abraham in the Hasidic Imagination* (Cincinnati, OH: Hebrew Union College, 1989), pp. 31ff.

Reading it in this other—and by no means entirely new— way—The notion of the *penimi,* or "inward," as the spiritual is a commonplace of Jewish religious literature since the Middle Ages. For some comments on the early history of this usage, cf. I. Twersky, *RaBaD of Posquieres* (Cambridge: Harvard University Press, 1962), p. 243, n. 16. "Inwardness" or "inward meaning" is sought in such diverse Jewish intellectual realms as philosophical exegesis (cf. the comments by F. Talmage in *Jewish Spirituality* I, pp. 313ff.) and mystical theology. The term has a particular prominence in the 'Iyyun circle of early kabbalists. See the edition and translation of 'Iyyun texts by M. Verman, *The Books of Contemplation: Medieval Jewish Mystical Sources* (Albany: SUNY, 1991), and Verman's discussion in connection with the so-called " 'Iyyun-short" text. The term passes into Hasidism through the usual later kabbalistic and pietistic writings. It is especially beloved by Judah Leib Alter of Ger (1847–1905), author of *Sefat Emet,* who builds his entire theology around the notion of inwardness and the "innermost point." I am presently preparing for publication a bilingual reader of key passages from the *Sefat Emet.* On the theology of Judah Leib Alter, see Yoram Jacobson, "Exile and Redemption in Gur Hasidism" in *Da'at* 2/3 (1978–79), pp. 175–215 (in Hebrew; henceforth indicated by H), and "Truth and Faith in Gur Hasidic Thought" in *Essays in Jewish Mysticism, Philosophy, and Ethical Literature Presented to Isaiah Tishby* (Jerusalem, Magnes 1986), pp. 593–616 (H).

p. 13

"The Compassionate One wants the heart"—*Sanhedrin* 106b
and RaSHI ad loc. It is the RaSHI version that is widely quoted later.

"Make a tabernacle that I may dwell within them"—Exodus
25:8. Spiritual allegorization of the tabernacle passages in Exodus is
an ancient tradition, first found in the works of Philo. See his *Life of
Moses* III and *Special Laws,* XIIff. In *Questions and Answers on Exodus*
2:51, he seems to refer to a tabernacle that lies within each individual Israelite. The reading of these chapters as spiritual allegory is
widespread in the *Zohar* and other Jewish spiritual writings of the
Middle Ages. Compare the treatment by Isaiah Tishby in *The
Wisdom of the Zohar* (New York: Oxford, 1987), vol. 3, pp. 867ff.
The recent dissertation of my student, Seth Brody, *Human Hands in
Heavenly Heights* (University of Pennsylvania, 1991) covers the
early kabbalistic understanding of the Tabernacle/Temple and especially the relationship between their understanding of the ancient
cult and inward prayer. A full treatment of this theme, including
discussion of both hasidic and modern materials in the context of
their earlier history, would be most enlightening.

The application of this verse to the individual ("within" each of
them) rather than to the people as a whole, is a commonplace of
later Jewish (and especially hasidic) homilists. Interestingly, its
earliest usage refers to the body rather than the soul, and is found in
Midrash ha-Gadol, ed. R. Margaliot (Jerusalem: Mossad Ha-Rav
Kook, 1956), p. 569. The *Zohar* (1:129a) connects an individualized
reading of this verse to the *mitsvah* of *tefillin:* the Jew who dons *tefillin*
makes himself into a tabernacle for God. R. Bahya to Exodus 25:9
seems to be already referring to this *Zohar* passage. The later
homilists who use this reading include Samuel Laniado, Tobias
Halevi, and others. This reading is mentioned with some reserve by

Moses Alshiekh (*Torat Moshe,* ed. Warsaw: J. G. Munk, 1879; 2:89a). Among hasidic authors, it is already found in Jacob Joseph of Polonnoye (see *Zofnat Pa'aneah,* ed. G. Nigal (Jerusalem: Institute for the Study of Hasidic Literature, 1989), p. 327.

p. 14

A different place—Here is the place to recall the rabbinic saying: "He [God] is the place of the world, and the world is not His place" (*Bereshit Rabbah* 68:9). See the discussions by Arthur Marmorstein, *The Old Rabbinic Doctrine of God* (London: Jews' College, 1927), and E. Urbach, *The Sages* (Jerusalem: Magnes, 1975). The phrase, and even the word *makom* ("place") as a name for God, has long been used to provide justification for a Jewish panentheism, the world included or "located" within the divine. Nothing other than that is intended in this book.

Different modes of the only Being there is—Though here I have deliberately sought a phrasing reminiscent of Leibniz, I am quite convinced that the entire edifice of Kabbalah points in this direction. "God" and "world" are related in kabbalistic thinking by a complex web of parallel structural features, patterns of mutual imitation, and powerful acts of willed interpenetration. All that exists "above" is reflected "below," and vice versa. The "upper" and "lower" are hardly two entirely separate realms at all when this web is laid on most thickly. Whatever separation continues to exist between them is the result of sin or of the as yet uncompleted status of redemption. This complex relationship between worlds could be documented by sources from the whole range of kabbalistic litera-ture, as it is basic to the entire kabbalistic way of thought. See now the interesting treatment of *Sod ha-Malbush: The Secret of the Garment in the Zohar,* by Dorit Cohen-Alloro (Jerusalem: Hebrew Univer-sity, 1987)(H). The author treats a tradition that views our world as the "garb"or outermost self of the divine. The "ascent of the worlds" that is the central object of devotion in the Lurianic Kabbalah is, essentially, the restoration of the cosmos to its premundane state as a monad. See the sources quoted and discussed by Moshe Idel in *Kabbalah, New Perspectives* (henceforth KNP; New Haven: Yale University Press, 1989), pp. 62ff.

"The heavens are the heavens of God"—Psalm 115:16.

p. 15

The midrashic tale of young Abraham—On the tale cf. L. Ginzberg, *Legends of the Jews,* (Philadelphia: Jewish Publication Society, 1913), vol. 1, pp. 213ff. and notes in vol. 5, pp. 218ff. This reading was suggested to me many years ago by the poem *"Elilim"* by David Frischmann.

Faith in this One . . . has long existed within Judaism—at least since the advent of Jewish neo-Platonism in the eleventh century, and especially in some of its mystical versions. I am aware that most neo-Platonists took care precisely not to include the material world within the realm of the One. This was, in part, an apologetic move, calculated to distinguish their unitive and highly abstract faith from a pantheism that would leave no room for individual identity and moral choice, so vital to the dialogic faith they had inherited from the biblical and rabbinic sources. But such a view was certainly also a way of remaining faithful to the spirit–matter duality of the Platonic tradition. Platonic dualism is quite thoroughly commingled with rabbinic moral teachings in the later Jewish ethical literature. In hasidic mysticism (based on some earlier attempts, to be sure), the material world is taken to be the dwelling place of God in the full sense or else to be illusory altogether, rather than to be an unredeemably coarse, though real, lower order of being. This leads to a breakdown of the distinction between matter and spirit, and an insistence that the divine is to be found within the corporeal world. Once the dualism of God–world is linked to that of spirit–matter, the collapse of the latter leads to a questioning of the former as well.

p. 16

I cannot abandon this term—Here I am paraphrasing Martin Buber's *Eclipse of God* (New York: Harper and Row, 1952), pp. 7ff. I agree with Buber on this matter. Later in this paragraph ("For the nondualist . . ."), I am, of course, quite far from Buber's later position and significantly closer to his earlier "mystical" essays that have long been a source of inspiration to me.

as though it were possible for me to stand outside—This is the reversal of a statement by the Maggid of Mezritch. Cf. his *Or Torah* (Brooklyn, 1960 [rep. Husiatyn, 1901?]), p. 1. Commenting on "Do not enter into judgment with us," in the *Seliḥot* liturgy (based on Psalm 143:2), he suggests that the verse asks God to stand outside us for the moment, as though that were possible, so that we might be given the experience of standing before God in judgment. See also the interpretation of "I, I am he" (Deuteronomy 32:39) in Idel, KNP p. 64, as well as various sources quoted in my "Hasidism: Discovery and Retreat," to which I have already referred.

p. 18

Y-H-W-H, the One of all being—This understanding of the name as formed from the verb H-Y-H is of ancient origin, and is clearly reflected in the Torah text itself. I refer to Exodus 3:13, where the term eHYeH as a "name" for God is clearly offered in association with the name Y-H-W-H and the verb "to be." See the comments by Nahum Sarna to this effect in *The JPS Torah Commentary* (Philadelphia: Jewish Publication Society, 1991), ad loc. For further discussion of these names in modern Biblical scholarship, see A. Murtonen, *A Philological and Literary Treatise on the Old Testament Divine Names* (Helsinki, 1952), pp. 65ff. The kabbalists certainly understand the name this way. See, for example, *Bahya* to Exodus 3:13 and Isaac Ibn Latif, *Tsurat ha-'Olam* (Vienna, 1860), p. 5. The latter source is discussed by Idel, KNP, p. 346, n. 287.

Of course, most nouns in Hebrew are formed from verbal stems, and any of these may be seen as the freezing of movement in order to create the illusion of a static reality, for the sake of "naming." But Y-H-W-H stands, as it were, at the head of this pyramid of language: the most impossible configuration of the most abstract of verbs.

"Thought does not grasp you at all"—This is from the *Petiḥat Eliyahu,* the "prayer of Elijah," *Tikkuney Zohar* 17a. This kabbalistic confession of faith is widely reprinted in prayerbooks. Most Sephardic and Oriental liturgies have it recited daily as an introduction to prayer, while the hasidic version of the Sephardic rite assigns it to Friday afternoon as a prelude to Shabbat. I could recommend no better introduction to Jewish mystical thought for the Hebrew reader than a study of this brief text with the commentary of Hillel Zeitlin, twentieth-century mystic and martyr of the Warsaw ghetto, published in his *Be-Pardes ha-Ḥasidut veha-Kabbalah* (Tel Aviv: Yavneh, 1960).

As consonants and as vowels—See the interesting treatment of this theme in early Kabbalah by H. Pedaya in *Jerusalem Studies in Jewish Thought* vol. 6:3–4 (1987) pp. 161, 172.

p. 19

I am attracted to its abstraction in the term "Being"—By far the most profound Jewish discussion of the relationship between God and Being is that by Michael Wyschograd in *The Body of Faith* (Minneapolis: Seabury, 1983), pp. 125ff. There is much that I learn from this chapter, despite some deep disagreements. Essentially, I find Wyschograd's theology overly biblical. He does not take cognizance of the deeply transformative recasting of the biblical legacy that took place in the wake of both philosophy and kabbalah. Ultimately, he tries to stake out a contemporary position reminiscent of that of Judah Halevi in his day: a passionate declaration of faithfulness to biblical personalism in the face of philosophical abstraction.

As will become clear in the following pages, I want to have it both ways in this regard, and I insist that is possible. In rejecting the identification of God with Being, Wyschograd says (p. 162): "But being is nevertheless not God. To be more precise, being is not Hashem." Hashem, for Wyschograd, refers to the personal God of the Bible. But strangely he does not mention the fact that Hashem, or "the Name" (he writes it in English as though it were a proper noun), is precisely a euphemism for Y-H-W-H, and the association of that, the *real* name, with Being cannot be ignored.

Despite this basic difference in approach, several of Wyschograd's strictures have been important to me. I insist that Y-H-W-H is ever the union of Being and Becoming, as the ongoing text makes clear, and also that it does remain the *name* of God, and not simply an abstraction.

p. 21

Speak My Name—The Bible's use of multiple terms and names for the deity has long been a subject of speculation and analysis. Midrashic authors sought to explain the meaning and origin of each name. Thus *Adonay* was attributed, as we shall see, to Adam, *Tseva'ot* to Hannah (*Berakhot* 31b), *Shaddai* was explained as "the One who said 'Enough!' to His world" (*Tanhuma Buber Lekh Lekha* 25), and so forth. The rabbis also accounted for the alternation between the two chief designations, Y-H-W-H and *Elohim,* as referring respectively to God's "Aspect of Mercy" and "Aspect of Justice." See the discussion by E. Urbach, op. cit. pp. 448ff. This latter approach opened the way for the kabbalists, who saw each of the divine names as a reference to one or another of the ten *sefirot.* The best guide to this reading of Scripture, in which the proper names are augmented by a host of other kabbalistic symbols, is Joseph Gikatilla's *Sha'arey Orah* (Hebrew ed. J. Ben-Shlomo, Jerusalem: Bialik Institute, 1981). It is interesting to note that the same alternation of names within the Torah text, so recognized by traditional scholarship as a source of significance, became the key by which the modern documentary hypothesis divided sections of the text into different presumed schools of authorship. Though much refined and moderated, this approach is still considered to be of value in contemporary biblical scholarship.

Elohim, the Hebrew generic term for "god," retains its original plural form even when referring to the one God of the Bible. It is also used in the biblical text to designate other gods, either in the singular or collectively. Its technical singular form *Eloha* is seen only rarely. Y-H-W-H, on the other hand, is used exclusively for the one universal God, the name by which Israel calls the true God. On the term *shem ha-meforash,* see Urbach, op. cit., chapter 7, n. 6, and the article by M. Gruenbaum quoted there.

In associating both the static and dynamic aspects of divinity with the name Y-H-W-H, I resist a temptation to follow the tradition that distinguishes between two aspects of the One by the use of two names, though that could have been done in any of several ways. My choice is to emphasize the oneness and ultimate indistinguishability of being and becoming.

"I will raise him up"—Psalm 91:14. The midrash on this Psalm (*Midrash Tehillim* 91:8) quotes Rabbi Pinhas ben Ya'ir as teaching:

"Why are the prayers of Israel in this world not answered? Because they do not know the *shem ha-meforash*. But in the future the blessed Holy One will tell them His name . . . and they will pray and be answered." I suggest that this passage can be read in either a magical or a humanistic vein, and that it reflects a bridging of these two that is a key to the rabbinic mindset. It is because of a real "person-to-person" intimacy with God that Israel is to have supernatural power in the future world. The two aspects of this "knowing God's name" must remain inseparable from one another. Is it too far-fetched to see a contemporary application of this principle in a view of education that would insist on the unity and integration of sciences and humanities? Science in this equation is the descendent of the magical, as Malinowski and others have so long pointed out. The scientist "knows the name," that is, achieves understanding of natural forces and a degree of control over them. But that selfsame name is also the bearer of universal soul, and only the sensitivities of the humanist will bare it to us. Without this, the knowledge of the scientist remains incomplete. (On the necessary unity of technical knowledge and spiritual awareness in the kabbalistic universe, see the comment on this same verse in *Zohar* 3:184a.)

"We will *pronounce Your name*"—This is from *barukh she-amar*. This phrase in the liturgy seems to be a reflection of Exodus 20:21: "In every place where I mention My name, I shall come and bless you." It seems likely that the text here has been emended, a copyist shrinking back from an earlier "In every place where *you* mention My name." Several early versions confirm this reading. See *Targum Yerushalmi* (frag.) and *Bahya* ad loc., as well as the note by N. Sarna, op. cit, p. 251, n. 69. See also *Sifre* Numbers 39 and *Sifre* Deuteronomy 62, including L. Finkelstein's comment ad loc. For probable evidence of the mentioning of God's name in esoteric Jewish circles of the early centuries, see G. Scholem, *Jewish Gnosticism* (New York: Jewish Theological Seminary of America, 1960), p. 108.

p. 22

Knowing someone's name means knowing personally—The religion of the biblical prophets clearly represents a shift in emphasis from the magical to the personal quality in the power of knowing God's name. God also knows Israel personally by calling them by name. That the magical side of name-power is not lost in Israel is witnessed by its strong reappearance in post-biblical Judaism, as witnessed both in the New Testament and in rabbinic sources. See the treatment by Urbach, op. cit., chapter 7, and the many sources quoted there.

The giving of names—The tale of Adam's naming the animals is found in *Bereshit Rabbah* 17:4. See parallels listed in Louis Ginzberg's *Legends of the Jews,* vol. 5, p. 83, n. 29. On the naming of God in this tale, see the following.

p. 23

Y-H-W-H . . . is . . . Israel's name for the One.—The special link of the Jewish people with this name is discussed by Mordecai Kaplan in *Judaism as a Civilization* (New York: Macmillan, 1934), pp. 352ff., and *The Meaning of God in Modern Jewish Religion* (New York: Reconstructionist Press, 1962), pp. 334ff.

We cannot speak of Y-H-W-H existing or not existing—See again the discussion by Wyschograd, op. cit., p. 151. I find the ontological argument, like all proofs for God's existence, to be an interesting but ultimately meaningless exercise.

p. 24

A memory of the lives we led—The consideration is almost a blasphemous one from our religious point of view. If we are to reenter the great stream of being, what need is there for individual consciousness to be maintained? Need the drop of water that flows into the sea retain its memory of life as a separate drop? See the sources in Idel, KNP, pp. 67ff.

"You remember the entire enterprise"—From the Rosh Hashanah liturgy.

Surely Y-H-W-H cannot be less than that which it has contained—This may be derived by implication from its converse, spelled out in the hasidic collection *Keter Shem Tov* (Brooklyn: Kehot, 1972), p. 31 #241: The image of humanity "was" present in God even before the first human was created, "since to the blessed God past and future are one." The same must be true of the future as well.

"And after all is ended, God alone will rule in awe"—This is from *Adon Olam,* an ancient hymn that opens the daily liturgy. This phrase offers a glimpse, rather rare in Jewish sources, of a final destruction of the universe. The historical worldview of the biblical–rabbinic tradition insisted that we could neither see backward before Creation nor see forward beyond the final redemption that was the goal of history. Our earliest esoteric traditions (the so-called *Ma'aseh Bereshit*) apparently broke the one taboo, but not the other. Most Jewish speculations on the ultimate future concluded with the resurrection of the dead, but refused to go farther. It was only the later philosophical and kabbalistic schools that took up this challenge, and then in a highly guarded way. Jewish Aristotelian philosophy saw the afterlife as the perfected mind's approach to union with the active Intellect, a union or identification that was never quite complete. Certainly the physical self had no role in such union. For Maimonides' controversial views on the nonpermanence of bodily resurrection, see his *Ma'amar Teḥiyat ha-Metim*

("Treatise on Resurrection"), and the introduction by Joshua Finkel (Proceedings of the American Academy for Jewish Research, New York, 1938–39) vol. 9, pp. 63ff., as well as Finkel's treatment in S. Baron's *Essays on Maimonides* (New York: AMS Press, 1966), pp. 93ff. The idea that all things eventually return to their source andthus cease to exist as separate beings is more comfortably a part of the neo-Platonic tradition. It appears in Kabbalah first in the writings of R. Ezra of Gerona. For a philosophic statement that spells out this reading of *Adon Olam,* see Bahya ben Asher to Numbers 10:35 (ed. Chavel, vol. 3, p. 57): "Since the entire Torah is built on the premise that the world has a beginning, it should be understood that it has an end as well. Indeed, anything that has a beginning must also have an end." Thus Scripture says: "I am first and I am last" (Isaiah 44:6). This Scripture indicates that the world has an end; just as God existed before all creatures, so will God exist after the last of them. Were any creature to remain in the world, God would not be last. As Chavel points out, in this matter, Bahya disagrees with Maimonides. See *Guide to the Perplexed* 2:27.

Among the most highly guarded secrets of the kabbalists was their belief in *shemitot,* or cosmic cycles of existence. Each of the seven lower *sefirot* was said to represent an aeon in which the universe existed. Our entire history, since creation, represents only the second of these seven aeons, the cycle of *din,* or divine justice. Our anticipated messianic age is actually just a transition into the new aeon, one in which the principle of glory *(tif'eret),* rather than justice (or law), will rule the world. At the end of the seventh cycle, often identified with the forty-nine thousandth year, will come a great cosmic jubilee, when the whole of Creation returns to the womb of the third *sefirah,* named "return" or "penitence," or even, according to some of the later kabbalists, to nothingness. On this idea, see G. Scholem, *On the Kabbalah and Its Symbolism* (New York: Schocken, 1965), p. 78; E. Gottlieb, *The Kabbalah in the Writings of R. Bahya ben Asher Ibn Halawa* (Jerusalem: Kiryath Sepher, 1970), pp.

233ff.(H); and the extended treatment by Israel Weinstock in his *Studies in Jewish Philosophy and Mysticism* (Jerusalem: Mossad Harav Kook, 1969), pp. 153–241(H). There is certainly a parallel, and perhaps even a historical link, between this worldview and aspects of Indian cosmology. Contemporary scientific views of the ultimate future of our universe lend interest to a reexamination of such traditions.

p. 25

"Today, if you listen to God's voice"—Psalm 95:7. This phrase, which appears in the first psalm of the *Kabbalat Shabbat* service, is also used by the rabbis to answer the question: "When will messiah come?" (*Sanhedrin* 98a).

p. 26

"My other half"—While this English expression is surely not of Jewish origin, the *Zohar* refers to an unmarried man as "half a body." See *Zohar* 3:7b and other sources quoted by I. Tishby in *Mishnat ha-Zohar* II (Jerusalem: Bialik Institute, 1961), p. 607. See also the extended discussion of this theme in Idel, KNP, pp. 62ff.

p. 27

Ecstatic outbursts—Such "outbreaks" of ecstasy supposedly happened among the hasidim in the days before "controls" were instituted. I refer especially to the descriptions of ḥasidey TaLK, the ecstatic outbursts that supposedly took place in 1770, as discussed in the ḤaBaD sources. Another early tale tells of a disciple who became so ecstatic in the ritual bathhouse that he entered the adjoining synagogue, when he heard the prayers had begun, and danced about for two hours before he realized that he had forgotten to put on his outer garments! (*Shivḥey ha-BeSHT,* ed. Horodezky; Berlin: Ajanoth, 1922, p. 57). A wonderful and highly authentic fictional evocation of these early heady days of the hasidic revival is found in the novel *Chaim Gravitser,* by Fischel Schneersohn (Berlin: Juedischer Literarischer Verlag, 1922). That interesting work still awaits translation into English.

Tsimtsum—A great deal has been written about this key concept of Kabbalah, which is understood somewhat differently in Hasidism. The best English explanation of the hasidic usage is that by Louis Jacobs in *Seeker of Unity* (New York: Basic Books, 1966), pp. 49ff.

Only bit by bit . . . are we allowed to peer—Traditional sources understand well the need for gradual initiation and enlightenment. See, for example, R. Bahya to Exodus 3, on the beginning of Moses' prophetic training.

p. 29

"Seek My face . . ."—"Your face, O Y-H-W-H, will I seek" Psalm 27:8.

"To behold the beauty . . ."—Psalm 27:4. See the rich treatment of these passages by Jon Levinson in *Sinai and Zion* (Minneapolis: Winston, 1985) or, in shorter form, in "The Jerusalem Temple in Devotional and Visionary Experience," included in JS I.

"Face to face, like a person with his neighbor"—Exodus 33:11.

"May God cause . . ."—Numbers 6:25–26.

When Moses comes down from the mountain—Exodus 34:29ff. For the aggadic discussion of this motif, see L. Ginzberg, *Legends of the Jews,* vol. 2, p. 143, and vol. 6, p. 61, n. 311; and M. Kasher, *Torah Shelemah,* ad loc.

An ancient poem—The reference is to the piyyut *Mar'eh Kohen,* recited in the Ashkenazic rite at the conclusion of the Avodah service on Yom Kippur. See text and translation in P. Birnbaum's edition of *The High Holyday Prayerbook* (New York: Hebrew Publishing, 1951), pp. 827ff. Of course, the sun itself is said in Psalm 19 to be as radiant as a bridegroom coming forth from his chamber!

Both prophet and priest—"When God chooses a prophet and shines *Shekhinah* upon him, the angel-of-the-face gives him the brilliance of *Shekhinah,* and his face is as radiant and glowing as the sun." *Sefer ha-Ḥeshek* (Lvov, 1865), p. 1.

We would follow Maimonides—*Guide to the Perplexed* 1:37.

p. 30

Rabbi Nahman Kossover—See the essay on him by Abraham Joshua Heschel translated in his *The Circle of the Ba'al Shem Tov* (Chicago: University of Chicago, 1985), pp. 113ff. The story is mentioned briefly on p. 118. I believe that I heard the version quoted here from Heschel.

Ever to contemplate the four-letter name—For the history of contemplating the name as a key devotional focus in Judaism, see M. Idel, KNP, pp. 50ff., p. 296, n. 97ff. and passim. Of course, this book is intended as just such a meditation.

p. 31

The teaching of Hillel—*Va-Yikra Rabbah* 34:3. In *Tosefta Berakhot* 4:1, the rabbis discuss whether one may use one's face, hands, or feet for anything *other* than the glory of God. See the discussion by S. Lieberman in *Tosefta Ki-Feshutah* (New York: Jewish Theological

Seminary of America, 1955) ad loc, who quotes this Hillel text in that connection. Lieberman reads Hillel's religious attitude as one that saw no conflict between serving the Creator's glory and taking reasonable pleasure at life in God's world.

p. 32

So the face is our gift to God—To use a rabbinic idiom, I am suggesting that the face of God—or the making over of the divine in human form—is a *keli maḥazik berakhah,* "a vessel to contain blessing." We are enabled to receive the flow of divine blessing through the "channel" we create by our projected images of the One.

Maimonides' claim—*Guide* 2:32ff. For a discussion of Maimonides' views of prophecy, see H. Kreisel, "Maimonides' View of Prophecy as the Overflowing Perfection of Man," *Da'at* 13 (1984) xxi–xxvi, and the extensive literature quoted there, including the essay by A. J. Heschel, "Did Maimonides Strive for Prophetic Inspiration?" in the *Louis Ginzberg Jubilee Volume,* Hebrew Section (New York: American Academy for Jewish Research, 1945).

The role of imagination—Maimonides' views stand behind the wonderful *Zohar* passage (1:103a–b), in which Proverbs 31:23 is interpreted as referring to "the gates of imagination," claiming that each person knows God only in accord with that which "he imagines in his heart." See the eye-opening comments by R. Shimon Lavi in *Ketem Paz* (Djerba: J. Haddad, 1940) ad loc, as well as the translation and commentary by D. Matt in *Zohar: the Book of Enlightenment* (New York: Paulist, 1983), pp. 65ff. I have previously discussed this passage in "The Role of Jewish Mysticism in a Contemporary Theology of Judaism," in *Conservative Judaism* 30:4, (1976) p. 20. Heschel also refers to it in *God in Search of Man* (New York: Harper 1955), p. 149.

For an interesting modern analogue, see the following passage by

Abraham Isaac Kook: "[Take care] not to switch the contents, mistaking a speculative concept for a scientific one, or an imaginary concept for a rational one, and so forth. For then you can be enticed by deception's web. But as long as one watches out for the border between perceptions, and knows how to move upward from the obvious to the secret (for the elevated matter of emanation can only be considered by way of speculation and imagining), one may find divine strength within the self. The sublime light will shine on such a person, for his path leads to God's presence." *Orot ha-Kodesh* 1 (Jerusalem: Mossad Ha-Rav Kook, 1984) pp. 218ff. Quoted in B. Ish-Shalom, *Ha-Rav Kook* (Tel Aviv: Am Oved, 1990), p. 49.

p. 33

The kabbalists refer to this insight in their distinction between *Eyn Sof*. . . and *sefirot*—See the extended discussion of *Eyn Sof* and *sefirot* in I. Tishby's *Wisdom of the Zohar,* vol. 1, pp. 230ff. and 269. The nature of the *sefirot* and their role as "masks" is discussed repeatedly throughout the history of kabbalistic literature. For the specific genre known as "Commentaries on the Ten Sefirot," see the bibliography by G. Scholem, "Index to Commentaries on the Ten Sefirot" (H), published as a supplement to *Kiryat Sefer,* vol. 10 (1934). From the fifteenth century onward, discussion of the *sefirot* more frequently becomes intertwined with treatment of divine attributes, as the philosophical and kabbalistic traditions are drawn together. Some of the more interesting later discussions are those by David Messer Leon, Moses Cordovero, and Joseph Ergas. See also the discussions by J. Ben-Shlomo in *Torat ha-Elohut shel R. Moshe Cordovero* (Jerusalem: Bialik Institute, 1965), pp. 72ff; Hava Tirosh-Rothschild, "Sefirot as the Essence of God in the Writings of David Messer Leon," *AJS Review* 7–8 (1982–83), pp. 409ff., and in her book *Between Worlds: The Life and Thought of Rabbi David Ben Judah Messer Leon* (Albany: State University of New York Press, 1991);

and Moshe Idel in KNP, p. 137ff., as well as in "Between the Views of Sefirot as Essence and Instruments in the Renaissance Period," *Italia* 3 (1982) pp. 89ff. (H). Of course, a contemporary neo-Kabbalah would want to base itself on those views that understood the *sefirot* as existing "from the side of the receivers," rather than having ontological status, while the latter is clearly the dominant view within the kabbalistic tradition. On the history of the phrase "from the side of the receivers," see Idel, KNP, p. 138, and the sources quoted there.

It is only from our limited point of view—Another bridge between the kabbalistic view of the *sefirot* as "reality" and our understanding of them (and of all images of God!) as projection might be built across the insights supplied by ḤaBaD, and especially by R. Aaron of Starroselje, who distinguishes "God's point of view" and "man's point of view" as two ways of viewing all of reality. A full clarification of these views in English by Rachel Elior will soon be available. The evolution of the notion of "point of view" from the neo-Platonic sources and the later kabbalists mentioned in the preceding note to its wider application in ḤaBaD thought would make an interesting subject for historical review.

There are two great moments—Cf *Mekhilta beshala shirta* 4, (ed. Horovitz-Rabin, p. 129) and parallels. See my treatment of this motif in "The Children in Egypt and the Theophany at the Sea" in *Judaism* 24:4 (1975).

A particularly startling hasidic interpretation—Quoted in the name of Abraham Joshua Heschel of Apt, by Zvi Hirsch of Zidachov in *Ateret Zvi, aḥarey mot* (ed. Jerusalem, 1960, 25a). See also the much earlier comment by Shabbatai Donnolo, tenth-century physician and religious thinker, that Ezekiel was shown the image of a man, a figure familiar to him, on the throne in his vision, lest he become too frightened by "the image of God as it really is," and die a sudden death. *Perush Na'aseh Adam,* ed. A. Jellinek (Leipzig, 1854), p. 2. See also *Sefer ha-Ḥeshek* (Lvov, 1865), section 25.

p. 34

Another old rabbinic source—*Bereshit Rabbah* 17:4.

Only when humans enter the scene—See *Pesaḥim* 50a: "In this world I am written Y-H-W-H but pronounced Adonay; in the next world it will be all one: written Y-H-W-H and pronounced Y-H-W-H." In the "next world"—whether that refers to the afterlife or to messianic times on earth—man's need for mastery–submission will no longer be in force.

p. 35

All the prophets but Moses—*Yebamot* 49b, and see RaSHI ad loc. A most important discussion of this passage, focusing on spiritual issues central to Judaism, is that by Judah ben Barzilai of Barcelona in his *Commentary to Sefer Yezirah* (Berlin: Mekize Nidramim, 1885), pp. 11ff.

One ancient midrash—See Abraham ben Eliezer of Bohemia (13th century), *Arugat ha-Bosem* (Jerusalem: Mekize Nirdamim, 1939–1963,) vol. 4, p. 59, n. 1. This source will be mentioned again in our chapter on revelation, in connection with the interpretive tradition of Proverbs 27:19, and the kabbalistic view of prophecy as encounter with the "higher" self.

p. 36

"No human may see Me and live"—Exodus 33:20.

"You will see My back . . ."—Exodus 23.

"They saw the God of Israel"—Exodus 24:10.

"Face to face"—Deuteronomy 34:10. Of course, I realize that I am taking this phrase more literally than it is often read. See *Likkutey MoHaRaN* 19:9.

"Those who see God"—Homiletically deriving *Yisra'el* from *shwr,* a root meaning "see." This insight is contained in the very interesting book, *Israel in Time and Space,* by Alexandre Safran (Jerusalem: Feldheim, 1987), p. 10. See the sources listed there.

This is a debate that accompanies Judaism throughout its history—See the important summary by G. Scholem in *The Mystical Shape of the Godhead* (New York: Schocken, 1991), pp. 1ff. See further, the extreme statement by Judah ben Barzilai of Barcelona (eleventh century; *Perush Sefer Yezirah,* p. 14), where he insists that even the thought that God has a form is idolatry. A similar statement by Maimonides is the object of R. Abraham ben David's famous objection to *Mishneh Torah, teshuvah* 3:7.

p. 37

"Peers out from the windows . . ."—Canticles 2:9.

p. 38

God the young lover and warrior—The clear identification of the youthful God-image of the Sea with God as lover is made by Judah ben Barzilai (*Perush Sefer Yezirah,* p. 137). This reference should supplement those mentioned in my article "The Children in Egypt," to which I have referred earlier.

The religion of Rabbi Akiva—Cf. Judah Goldin's "Toward a Profile of the Tanna, Aqiba ben Joseph," in his *Studies in Midrash and Related Literature* (Philadelphia: Jewish Publication Society, 1988), pp. 299ff. Compare also my previous discussion in "The Song of

Songs in Early Jewish Mysticism" in *Orim: A Jewish Journal at Yale* 2:2 (1987), pp. 49ff.

"Had the Torah not been given . . ."—*Aggadat Shir Ha-Shirim,* ed. S. Schechter (Cambridge, England: Deighton Bell & Co., 1896), line 22.

p. 39

Some have attributed it to a totemic emasculation—Thus, Richard Rubenstein in *After Auschwitz* (Indianapolis: Bobbs-Merrill, 1966).

p. 40

"Half a form"—I refer to a homily by Dov Baer of Mezritch on Numbers 10:2, in which *shtey hatsotserot kesef* ("two silver trumpets") is read as *shtey hatsi tsurot . . . kissuf.* These two half forms, according to the Maggid of Mezritch, are God and the self, each of whom is incomplete without the other, and therefore filled with longing (*kissuf* instead of *kesef*). *Maggid Devaraw Le-Ya'aqov,* ed. R. Schatz (Jerusalem: Magnes, 1976), p. 38. Cf. Idel, KNP, p. 65.

Kabbalah in its fullest development—See I. Tishby, op. cit. vol. 1, pp. 371ff. and elsewhere; also the brief treatment in my essay on the Song of Songs, to which I have previously referred.

p. 41

As this genre of Jewish creativity becomes open—I first suggested this in an essay entitled "Bride, Spouse, Daughter: Images of the Feminine in Classical Jewish Sources," published in S. Heschel's *On Being a Jewish Feminist* (New York: Schocken, 1983), pp. 248ff.

The eternal search for unity—I have found these remarks echoed in a remarkable but generally unknown treatise called *Ha-Torah veha-Avodah* (Piotrkow, 1909), p. 51 by Joseph H.Y. Studienizke, a rabbi in Kharkov at the turn of the century.

p. 42

As the dualities of God and world ... are meant to be overcome, so too is the duality of male and female—I might even go so far as to say that the relationship of *sovev* and *memale* is an understood *covenant;* both sides know that their duality is somehow playacting, and that ultimate truth lies in their unity. So too male and female. Might this be why the incision of Israel's *brit* is in the flesh of the gender-defining organ, showing that its assertion of difference is not so total after all?

"There is no man without woman. . . ."—*Bereshit Rabbah* 8:8.

p. 43

Unity exists only in fleeting moments—It is generally the way of Jewish spirituality to accept this reality; I see that realism as one of its strengths. The ebb and flow of spiritual insight is often referred to as *ratso va-shov,* "running back and forth," based on Ezekiel 1:14. I have discussed this long ago in an essay entitled "Toward a Theology of Jewish Spirituality" in *The New Jews,* ed. A. Mintz and J. Sleeper, New York: Vintage Press, 1971.

A rare exception to this view is R. Levi Yizhak's treatment of Moses, quoted by Idel in KNP, p. 310, n. 123. There, Moses is viewed as a permanently "enlightened one," in classic "Eastern" fashion.

p. 44

The Ba'al Shem Tov was told—In the conversation with messiah that took place during a "soul-ascent" in 1746. The Ba'al Shem Tov reports this event in the famous letter to his brother-in-law, Gershon Kitover. This letter is translated in L. Jacobs' *Jewish Mystical Testimonies* (New York: Schocken, 1977), pp. 148ff.

Yod is the point of departure—The kabbalists associate *Yod* with *ḥokhmah,* or primal wisdom, the second of the ten *sefirot.* Its tip ever points silently upward toward that which is beyond it, *keter,* the crown or the first emanation. See *Zohar* 3:106, 65b. But see also the interesting text from *Sha'arey Tsedek,* quoted by Idel in KNP, p. 63. There the human being is a *Yod,* parallel to, and fulfilling the divine *Yod.* Folk tradition has it that the two *Yods,* often used in writing to abbreviate the name of God, stand for two Jews (Yiddish: *tsvey yudn/tsvey yidn*), for wherever two Jews meet for the purpose of Torah, the *Shekhinah* dwells with them. But could the two *Yods* be God and the person? Could God and person, each a *Yod,* be joined together in a single Aleph? This is suggested by R. Menahem Nahum of Chernobyl in *Me'or Eynayim, bereshit* (in my English translation, *Upright Practices and the Light of the Eyes* (New York: Paulist Press, 1982), pp. 80ff.

p. 45

Torah, our teaching, is the name of God—The daily blessing for Torah-study reads "May we, our children, and our children's children all *know Your name and study Your Torah* for its own sake." (Emphasis mine.)

CREATION

p. 51

A seated deity . . . contrasted by dancing gods—I owe this characterization of the dichotomy to a long-ago conversation with Leonie Sachs.

God is both the source and the flow, the hidden root and the endless branches—My views on the unity of all being are close in many ways to those of Rabbi Abraham Yizhak ha-Kohen Kook, though they have been arrived at independently. For Kook on the unity of all being, see B. Ish Shalom, *Ha-Rav Kook* (Tel Aviv: 'Am 'Oved, 1990), pp. 208ff. See also his comments on two types of perfection, quoted in ibid., pp. 62ff.

p. 52

"World" is the universe seen in its outward garb—See Sallie McFague, "The World as God's Body," in her *Models of God* (Philadelphia: Fortress Press, 1987), pp. 69ff. For some earlier Christian views of the world as the body of God, based partly on exegesis of Collosians 1:17, see the discussion by Idel in KNP, pp. 116ff.

p. 55

A religious language that speaks of the underlying unity—My thinking on this subject has been stimulated by Thomas Berry's *The Dream of the Earth* (San Francisco: Sierra Club, 1988). I am grateful to Steve Shaw for directing me to that book, along with several others. Berry's call upon those of us who still live in "numinous communities" to expand our notion of community and fellow-feeling beyond the human realm to embrace all species and forms of life finds a responsive chord in me. I do so in the highly particular-istic language of Judaism, but the intent is fully universal. I believe that humanity will best approach this universal fellow-feeling through a deep turning toward, and then a sharing of, our many particularist traditions.

I know that the creation cycle has happened in my life once again—There have been periods when the daily recitation of each day's creation has played a key role in my prayer life. This practice (i.e., reciting "In the beginning. . . ." on Sunday morning, "God said: 'Let there be a firmament' " on Monday, and so forth) has ancient roots in Judaism, associated with prayers offered in support of the daily morning sacrifices in the Temple. See *Mishnah Ta'anit* 4:3. These so-called *ma'amadot* can still be found in the back pages of some traditional prayerbooks. The cycle of recitation then culminates in the words "Heaven and earth were finished" at the beginning of *kiddush* on Friday evening.

p. 56

Rabbi Nahman tells the tale of a prince—This is the introduction to his famous *Seven Beggars.* See the Band translation of *The Tales* (New York: Paulist Press, 1978), p. 256.

p. 57

To see the two tales as versions of the same story, representing two stages in humanity's own evolving self-understanding—I would suggest a more specific parallel as well. Genesis 1 is a harmonistic tale, one in which the single God creates and unifies heaven and earth. Biblical scholars have long pointed out that this tale represents a significant development from the pre-biblical and earlier Israelite versions of the story, in which Creation was but the culmination of the primal battle between gods and cosmic forces (See John Day, *God's Conflict with the Dragon and the Sea;* Cambridge, England: Cambridge University Press, 1985). Elements of these earlier mythical tales are preserved in Scripture, especially in certain passages of the Psalms. *I am suggesting that the same process of harmonization, a crucial step forward in humanity's intellectual–spiritual development, needs to take place again in our day.* We are now heirs to a new account of origins, but one that sees us emerging out of biological rather than mythical chaos, survivors of an endless war among the species. Like the inspired author of Genesis I, we too will have to overcome this legacy of chaos and create of it a vision of harmony. Since we Jews are the special heirs of those who did this last time around in Western history, surely we should seek some involvement this time as well.

p. 58

This priority is essentially one of primitive logic—Cf. Wyschograd (*The Body of Faith,* p. 136): "Being is prior to beings, not in the temporal but in the ontological sense."

Rather than one of time—For a different (and more "ontological") concept of both time and space within Judaism, see the early kabbalistic sources discussed by I. Weinstock in *Studies in Jewish Philosophy and Mysticism* (H) pp. 170ff.

p. 59

Creation as emanation—This rereading of the biblical account of Creation has a long history in Judaism. It is especially associated with neo-Platonic thought. For a brief discussion of emanation and its place in medieval Judaism, see the treatments by J. Kramer and G. Scholem in the *Encyclopaedia Judaica* 6:694ff, s.v. "emanation." Emanation plays a key role in all of kabbalistic thought, where mystical devotion or "ascent" is essentially viewed as a reversal of the emanation process. In both philosophy and kabbalah, however, there is hesitation when it comes to accepting the *material* world as a divine emanation. The antimaterialist bias is also a part of the Platonic legacy. Hasidic thought inherits the language of emanation from earlier Jewish mysticism, but does not allow for this absolute distinction between the upper and lower worlds. The corporeal world itself is the "garb" of God. It is for this reason that Buber embraces Hasidism as the first Western mysticism that has been able to shed the gnostic burden of antiworldliness. See the note on p. 5 of the preceding chapter.

p. 60

The *ayin* out of which being emerged—See the remarkable descriptions of kabbalistic emanation theory in G. Scholem's *Major Trends in Jewish Mysticism* (New York: Schocken Books, 1954), pp. 217ff., and *On the Kabbalah and Its Symbolism* (New York: Schocken Books, 1969), pp. 100ff. For a fuller discussion of mystical nothingness in Judaism, see D. Matt's "Ayin: The Concept of Nothingness in Mystical Judaism" in *The Problem of Pure Consciousness,* ed. Robert Forman (Oxford, England: Oxford University Press, 1990).

p. 61

A word closely related to the name of God—According to *Zohar* 1:16b, *yehi* itself is a divine name.

The world is born, rather than spoken, out of God.—I refer here to the kabbalistic lore around *binah,* the third of the ten *sefirot,* often described as supernal mother and source of inner divine birth. See the discussion and examples provided by Tishby in *The Wisdom of the Zohar,* vol. 1, pp. 281ff., p. 341, and Scholem's essay on "Shekhinah: The Feminine Element in Divinity" in his *On the Mystical Shape of the Godhead* (New York: Schocken, 1991).

Here we are called to take note of the first letter *Heh* of the divine name—And the rabbis say that this world was created with a *Heh!* Cf. *Midrash Tehillim,* ed. S. Buber, p. 307; *Bereshit Rabbah* 12:10. This idea is interestingly developed in *Otiot de-Rabbi Akiva* (S. Wertheimer, Battey Midrashot, vol. 2, Jerusalem: Mossad Ha-Rav Kook, 1953, p. 363), where *Heh* is identified with the entire divine name.

p. 62

Contemplation, says the father of all kabbalists—Rabbi Isaac the Blind, *Commentary on Sefer Yetsirah* (in G. Scholem, *Ha-kabbalah Be-Provence,* Jerusalem: Mifal ha-Shikhpul Stenograph, 1963, p. 1, ll. 15–16).

Whichever of these two accounts we use—Behind my use of kabbalistic language, there lies a mostly unspoken assumption that our mystics had some cosmological ideas, however highly imperfect and primitively articulated, that correspond to reality. I do not find this entirely shocking from an epistemological point of view. The human mind, product of countless generations of evolutionary development, contains within it the record or trace of each of these generations. As the mystic—using the techniques handed down in any of the great traditions—learns to strip away outer layers of consciousness and penetrate into deeper mind, why should he or she not come away with some sense of the cosmic process as it is embedded with the mind? Thus, I would claim that the correspondence between macrocosm and human microcosm, so long held dear by esoteric traditions throughout the world, indeed has a basis in reality that may one day be scientifically demonstrable.

Here, perhaps unlike the human analogy, separation is only superficial—See *Tanya* 2:2.

p. 63

If all is one . . . why do we experience life as so fragmented?— Jewish mystics in all generations have sought answers to this question. The theory that underlies *sefirot* in early kabbalah may be seen as an attempt to respond to this question by graduating it, that is, by showing the infinitely gradual and complex steps by which the One became or gave forth the many. *Tsimtsum,* both in its Lurianic and hasidic versions, is also an attempted response to this question, rephrased as "If the One is all, how is there room for the many?" A third response is that which the kabbalists refer to as *sod 'iq* or *alef-yod-quf,* the secret of 1-10-100. The decade of the *sefirot* is but a repetition of the primal monad; only a zero has been added. Thus the ten are truly only one, but just raised to the next power. The same is true of one hundred, one thousand, and so forth. This "secret" may be described as a mathematical response to a theological problem. On the ancient roots of this discussion see Idel, KNP, pp. 119ff. Here we have to posit some early (or even primal) meeting between Gnostics and neo-Pythagoreans.

Tsimtsum and *hitpashtut,* or divine contraction and divine flow—I use the terms as they are employed in the hasidic (and especially ḤaBaD), rather than the earlier kabbalistic, sources. For further explanation, I commend the reader to the writings of Rachel Elior, to which I have referred in the preceding chapter.

p. 65

Searching for the other . . . longing for fulfillment—This sense of a world order based on *ga'agu'im,* or deep and ultimately inexpressible longings for the restoration of cosmic unity, lies at the very core of the religious worldview of Bratslav Hasidism. See the nonpersonified portrayal of this longing and its tragic dimensions in Rabbi Nahman's parable of the "Heart of the World," quoted in my *Tormented Master,* p. 301. For a much earlier kabbalistic view similar to that expressed here, see the text of Rabbi Abraham ben David of Posquières, quoted by G. Scholem in *Reshit ha-kabbalah* (Jerusalem: Schocken, 1948) p. 79.

p. 67

The kabbalists responded to Maimonides—With apologies for oversimplification. I strongly believe (with Idel) that kabbalistic attitudes toward the *mitsvot* are rooted in ancient mythical views held by the rabbis, and are a natural outgrowth and schematization of an earlier Jewish gnosis. It was because of their deep attachment to such views, particularly of the commandments, that kabbalists took such a leading role in the anti-Maimonidean polemics.

p. 68

In a nondualistic worldview, the sharp edges are taken off this debate—In a truly monistic context, the center is *reality,* which is only One. It is at once Self and self; God, world, and soul. The ensuing pages may be seen as part of the "educational" process to which I referred at the end of the preceding chapter: the soul may know this truth, but the task is to find a way to put it so that the dualistic mind of *katnut,* or ordinary consciousness, may begin to absorb the message.

p. 69

The Psalmist. . . . another Psalm—The references are to Psalms 148 and 104.

p. 72

Haviv Adam she-nivra ba-tselem—*Avot* 3:14.

Nowhere is this more manifest—Again, the parallel to Rav Kook is clear. Here there is a perhaps surprising convergence between Kook's views and those of Mordecai M. Kaplan, an evolutionist coming from another direction. Both are striving for a Jewish religious evolutionism, one that should be developed in consideration of the writings of Teilhard de Chardin and his school. But so, too, is the Hegelian echo of such expressions: all of existence as ongoing dialectical self-revelation of "absolute spirit" does have an address in the Western philosophical tradition. In our century, it is carried on in the writings of Sartre, Heidegger, and others.

p. 73

". . . on a path between fields of fire and fields of ice"—*Tosefta Hagigah* 2:5.

Were we any closer. . . . any farther.—Thus did Rabbi Simhah Bunem of Przysucha understand the divine name *Shaddai* (or "just enough"): the one who revealed just enough so that humans, by stretching to the full extent of their powers, could find God. See R. Zadok ha-Kohen of Lublin, *Peri Tsadik* vol. 1 (part 2), 1b.

p. 74

The modalities of revelation and redemption—This seems an appropriate place to acknowledge the Rosenzweigian structure that has obviously influenced this work. My contact with Rosenzweig's thought began with my teacher, Nahum Glatzer; it is primarily the third part of the *Star,* some shorter essays (especially "The Builders"), and Glatzer's *Franz Rosenzweig: His Life and Thought* (New York: Schocken Books, 1961) that have been significant to me. More recently, I have come to read and appreciate Rosenzweig again through the writings of Paul Mendes-Flohr and Rivka Horwitz. Of course, I recognize a significant distance between my blatantly immanentist neo-kabbalism and Rosenzweig's much more guarded attitude toward mysticism.

Action must be joined to them—Here I am adding to the Rosenzweigian schema another triad from our classical sources: *Maḥashavah* or thought corresponds to Creation (the divine intention for existence), *dibbur* or speech to Revelation, and *ma'aseh* or deed to Redemption.

p. 75

But a new *halakhah* will only proceed from a new *aggadah*— Here, I am much influenced by the use of these categories in Hayyim Nahman Bialik's classic essay "Halakhah and Aggadah."

Jews have lost the art of thinking richly. . . .—Credit for a call to renew Midrash as a vehicle for contemporary Jewish theology goes to Emil Fackenheim. See his *God's Presence in History* (New York: New York University Press, 1970), pp. 20ff.

p. 76

All *mitsvot* exist for the same purpose—My views on the origin of the *mitsvot* are laid out in the next chapter. But the reader will already understand that the monistic vision, if carried forward to this realm, will also serve as a softening to the dualistic question: "Are the *mitsvot* of divine or of human origin?" Of course, my answer to that question will be "Yes."

The increased realization of divinity—The theory of *mitsvot* here also owes something to Kabbalah. Cf. *Ma'arekhet ha-Elohut* f. 94–95. An important discussion of *mitsvot* in Kabbalah is that by Daniel Matt ("The Mystic and the Mitzvot") in *Jewish Spirituality* I.

p. 78

The first *mitsvah:* be aware—Here, I am influenced by Maimonides' placing of the *mitsvah* to know God at the beginning of his list. My reading of Deuteronomy 4:39, which I believe to be original, has as its background the readings in Meir Ibn Gabbai's *Avodat ha-Kodesh* 1:11 and *Tanya* 2:1 and 6.

A combination of spontaneity and discipline—This is perhaps the most important practical teaching of my revered teacher, Abraham Joshua Heschel. He understood both the pure spontaneity that lies at the core of true prayer or religious life and the need for discipline to stimulate and protect it. See his *God in Search of Man* (New York: Harper, 1966), pp. 343ff., and at greater length in *Man's Quest for God* (New York: Scribner's, 1954), pp. 47ff. and passim.

The Ba'al Shem Tov . . . is said to have warned his disciples— *Tsava'at RYVaSH* (Cracow, 1896), 3a. Translated in A. Green and B. W. Holtz, *Your Word Is Fire* (New York: Paulist Press, 1977), p. 30.

p. 79

When Rabbi Akiva claimed—*Yerushalmi Nedarim 9:4.*

All the decisions we make in the interpersonal realm need to bear this principle in mind—This aggadic principle, I am claiming, forms the basis for a great deal of our *halakhah*. By the latter term I mean both traditionally received religious praxis *and* our own decision making for our lives. The aggadic principle also stands as a fixed point within our Judaism from which to evaluate and criticize traditional practice and advance its development to better meet the aggadic goal. The present-day call for egalitarian treatment of men and women in Jewish life stands on this reading of Genesis 5:1. A change in thinking about men and women in our time has called forth a new *aggadah.* This new *aggadah,* in turn, makes demands upon the *halakhah* by which we will live.

p. 81

"There is no person who does not have his hour"—*Mishnah Avot* 4:3.

p. 82

The Sabbath is surely the greatest gift—I have written about *Shabbat* in "Twin Centers: Sacred Time and Sacred Space" (*Recon-*

structionist 55:5, 1990, pp. 16ff.) and "Sabbath and Temple: Some Thoughts on Space and Time in Judaism," in *Go and Study: Essays and Studies in Honor of Alfred Jospe,* ed. R. Jospe and S. Z. Fishman, (Washington DC: B'nai B'rith Hillel, 1980), pp. 287ff. Accompanying the *Reconstructionist* piece (p. 22), I offer some simple beginning guidelines for the observance of a contemporary *Shabbat.*

p. 84

The rabbis tell us that shortly after Adam was created—*Kohelet Rabbah* 7:28.

The love of all God's creatures—Here, following the call of Thomas Berry and others, I am expanding the meaning of *briyot* beyond its usual reference of "people" to the more literal "creatures." The way to God is through the world; this includes both the path of human love and a compassionate embrace of all Creation.

p. 85

The ways we dispose of them—Here, I cannot help recall Rabbi Nahman's scatological image of the *tsaddik* who sits next to his own huge refuse heap, surely a prescient parody of our times if ever there was one! See Band's translation of *The Tales,* p. 274 and my brief treatment in *Tormented Master,* pp. 362ff.

p. 87

I believe the time has come—Sources on *Judaism and Vegetarianism* have been collected by Richard Schwartz (Marblehead, MA: Micah, 1988).

p. 89

We must shoo a mother bird away—Deuteronomy 22:6.

A mother and her calf—Leviticus 22:28.

p. 91

The rabbis say that whoever takes a human life negates the divine image—*Tosefta Yebamot* 8. R. Jacob Zemah notes that the word *kamokha* ("as yourself" in the phrase "Love your neighbor as yourself") is numerically one less than the following phrase "I am the Lord," showing that "If you harm one [person], you harm the Other, for 'the human was made in the image of God.' " *Shulḥan Arukh ha-ARIZaL* (Jerusalem, 1961), p. 27.

Among the hasidic teachings—Mordecai Joseph of Izbica, *Mey ha-Shiloaḥ*, Kedoshim.

"When God created the world"—*Bereshit Rabbah* 8:4, 12:15, etc.

p. 93

Did God create the world out of loving free will, or out of necessity?—This debate goes on throughout medieval Jewish philosophy. Even Ibn Gabirol, perhaps the most blatantly neo-Platonist of Jewish philosophers, has to introduce an element of will into the system in order to bring emanation into harmony with the free-willed God of the Bible. The parallel discussion in kabbalistic circles is around *keter,* usually seen as the first emanation, and its role as the primal will of God.

I trust that the intimations of faith in divine will are sufficiently clear in this volume, especially in this and the next chapter. I do see divine will manifest in the struggle toward consciousness that motivates and structures the entirety of evolution. As to whether Creation itself was an act of will, I feel too awed to answer. Here we stand at the other side of a black hole, after all. Surely that hole is parallel to the chamber of *ayin* or primal nothingness in Kabbalah. There is nothing I can say about the One that stands on the other side of that primal place.

See also the interesting recasting of these questions by Nahman of

Bratslav, in *Likkutey MoHaRaN* 52 and 65, as well as my discussions of it in *Tormented Master,* appendix I.

p. 94

But as humans we are here to direct that flow of life—Thomas Berry (*The Dream of the Earth,* p. 19) suggests to me that we have, in fact, reached a new stage in the evolution of our entire planet, as processes that were once guided by nature alone have now been taken over by humans—both by human wisdom and human folly. Deforestation and rape of the planet's resources are the work of conscious humans, as are decisions to protect a particular species or clean up a particular body of water. We are truly the hands in control of earth's survival, as Berry would say, so we *had better be* the compassionate hands of Y-H-W-H. Otherwise, there is no hope at all!

Those great keys—*Ta'anit 2a.*

Yod Heh is only half a name—Kabbalistic *kavvanot* for prayer and *mitsvot* include the phrase "to unite *Yod Heh* with *Vav Heh.*" Now you know why. *Yod Heh* for the kabbalist represents *ḥokhmah binah,* the cosmos at the threshold of inner divine birth, but not yet actualized. This is not yet a world in which *mitsvot* have a place.

REVELATION

p. 102

Yod Heh is indeed a divine name on its own—On the concluding verse of the Psalter, the rabbis comment: "Since the Temple has been destroyed, it suffices to praise God with two letters [*Yod Heh,* rather than the entire name]" *Eruvin* 18b. In the future, the full name will be restored.

God becomes word as we become human—Word, not flesh. The theology proposed here is not incarnational in the Christian sense, but has in common with Christian incarnationalism the central recognition of human distinctiveness.

p. 103

Bound in embrace like the cherubim over the Ark—*Yoma* 54a. Cf. A. J. Heschel, *Torah min ha-Shamayim* I (London: Soncino Press, 1962) pp. 62ff.

Divine speech is made accessible to us only through the human vessel—The rabbinic sources for this position have been collected and discussed by Heschel in op. cit., II, pp. 264ff.

p. 104

If revelation and commandment are the heart of Jewish faith—For some background on the treatment of these key motifs in twentieth-century Jewish thought, the reader might want to consult the important essays of Paul Mendes-Flohr and Rivka Horwitz in *Jewish Spirituality* II. The Horwitz essay is especially interesting in this context, showing that the key "dialogic" Jewish theologians of this century, Martin Buber and Franz Rosenzweig, both tend toward mysticism in their discussions of revelation.

p. 105

A well-known midrash—*Mekhilta Yitro, ba-hodesh* 5 (ed. Horovitz-Rabin, p. 221).

p. 107

For Maimonides and those who followed him—For a recent treatment of Maimonides' views of prophecy, see the article by H. Kreisel to which I have referred earlier. (p. 212)

A revelatory event is virtually assured—See A. Altmann, "Maimonides and Thomas Aquinas: Natural or Divine Prophecy?" in his *Essays in Jewish Intellectual History* (Hanover NH: University Press of New England, 1981) pp. 99ff.

The ecstatic mystics who followed in Maimonides' path—See the important treatment of this theme in Moshe Idel, *The Mystical Experience in Abraham Abulafia* (Albany NY: SUNY, 1988), and especially chapter three, which is vital background for the present treatment. The medievals reinterpreted biblical prophecy as an inner revelatory event resulting from patient training of the mind and rigorous contemplative discipline, phenomena that existed in their own day. In effect, the prophetic experience is thus reread as a mystical one, all modern distinctions between these (Heiler, etc.) notwithstanding. On mysticism as prophecy, compare Idel, op. cit., pp. 138ff. For an earlier medieval attempt to distinguish mystical (*merkavah*) experience from prophecy, see Judah ben Barzilai, *Commentary to Sefer Yetsirah*, p. 22.

p. 108

All the prophets but Moses saw "through a darkened glass"— *Yebamot* 49b; *Va-Yikra Rabbah* 1:14. See the extended discussions of this *aggadah* in Judah ben Barzilai, op. cit., pp. 11ff. The view that this "darkened glass" is a mirror is seen by some as evidence of an ancient technique of acquiring knowledge, allegedly used by the prophets. This claim is made in the literature of Ashkenazic pietism in the thirteenth century. See *Ḥokhmat ha-Nefesh* (Lvov, 1876), 29c, and reference in *Sefer ha-Navon,* in J. Dan, *Studies in Ashkenazi-Hasidic Literature* (Ramat Gan, Israel: Masada, 1975), p. 119 (H). For a kabbalistic comparison of prophecy to seeing in a mirror, see Judah Hayyat's commentary to *Ma'arekhet ha-Elohut*, ed. Mantua 143a. This passage is quoted at length by Isaiah Horowitz of Prague in *Shney Luḥot ha-Brit* (Jerusalem, 1959; offset of ed. Warsaw), vol. 2, p. 133, and thus was known to later, including hasidic, thinkers.

Prophetic revelation is the discovery of a deeper self—See G. Scholem's treatment of this theme in "Eine Kabbalistische Erklaerung der Prophetie als Selbstbegegnung" in Monatsschrift für Geschichte und Wissenschaft des Judenthums 74 (1930), pp. 285ff., and in "Tselem: The Concept of the Astral Body," now translated in his *On the Mystical Shape of the Godhead*.

Who thought they could recreate prophecy with proper inner training—Cf. A. J. Heschel, "Did Maimonides Strive for Prophetic Inspiration?" in the *Louis Ginzberg Jubilee Volume,* Hebrew Section (New York: American Academy for Jewish Research, 1945), pp. 159ff. On the recasting of biblical prophecy as mystical experience, see also the text by the hasidic thinker, Y. Y. Safrin, quoted by Idel in KNP, p. 95 (322, n. 143).

"In the voice of Moses"—*Berakhot* 45a. I recognize that the Talmud, and especially *Tosafot* ad loc, understands this phrase somewhat differently.

The *only* voice heard at Sinai was that of Moses—See Abraham Ibn Ezra's startlingly radical formulation: "For the speaker is a man and the hearer is a man." *Yesod Mora,* chapter 12, ed. Stern (Prague, 1833; 43a).

A moment in which the divine and human minds flow together—This was true of both Aristotelian and neo-Platonic theories of prophecy in the Middle Ages. On the adaptation of both of these into Jewish mysticism, see Idel, KNP, pp. 39ff.

p. 109

It takes a Moses to translate—A reversal of the passage just quoted from *Berakhot* 45a. Here, Moses is God's *meturgeman,* a relationship surely more to be expected than its opposite!

Later accounts of the revelation—See the many sources collected in L. Ginzberg, *Legends of the Jews,* vol. 3, pp. 109ff. and notes.

p. 112

Israel "saw the audible and heard the visible"—*Mekhilta Yitro ba-hodesh* 9 (235).

The free flow of inner energies—Rav Kook, who fully understood that prophecy and holy spirit are inward gifts, seeks to maintain a different status for the revelation of Torah itself. See Ish-Shalom, *Ha-Rav Kook,* pp. 72ff.

p. 113

"I shall be that I shall be" is interpreted by the rabbis—*Sh'mot Rabbah* 3:6; *Berakhot 9b.*

Torah as the Name of God—See the discussions by G. Scholem in "The Meaning of the Torah in Jewish Mysticism" in his *On the Kabbalah and Its Symbolism,* pp. 32ff., and "The Name of God and the Linguistic Theory of the Kabbala" in *Diogenes* 79 and 80 (1972).

p. 115

The kabbalists spoke of the entire Torah as the name of God—See the famous statement of this by Nahmanides in the introduction to his Torah commentary, quoted by Scholem in the former of the last-mentioned articles. On the relationship between Torah as name(s) of God, visionary experience, and contemplation of the *shi'ur komah* (the "bodily" form of God), see Idel, "The Concept of Torah in Heikhalot Literature and Its Metamorphoses in Kabbalah" in *Jerusalem Studies in Jewish Thought* v. 1 (1981), pp. 23ff. (H). See especially the passage from Gikatilla quoted on p. 61, where the name Y-H-W-H represents God stripped of all garments, the externals of Torah. The hasidic masters were influenced by passages like this, and go the further (or perhaps less precise) step of including the phenomenal world among the "garments" of God, which need to be stripped away in the highest moments of religious perception.

Maximalist and minimalist views—The same terms are used by my teacher David Weiss Halivni, "On Man's Role in Revelation" in *From Ancient Israel to Modern Judaism: Essays in Honor of Marvin Fox,* ed. J. Neusner et al (Atlanta: Scholars' Press, 1989), vol. 2, pp. 29ff. Halivni uses the categories somewhat differently, as he is examining only rabbinic sources, whereas I am ranging more widely through the history of Judaism. Of course, the rabbinic aspect of this discussion is all based on volume two of A. J. Heschel's *Torah min ha-Shamayim,* especially pp. 264ff.

They even discuss whether Moses at Sinai—See Heschel, op. cit., pp. 381ff.

"Everything a faithful student is ever to say. . . ."—Talmud Yerushalmi *Peah* 17a. Cf. Heschel, op. cit., pp. 234ff.

p. 116

"There is *nothing* that has not been hinted at in the Torah"—*Zohar* 3:221a and freq., based on *Ta'anit* 9a.

Only two commandments out of the mouth of the divine Dynamis—*Pesikta Rabbati* 22 (ed. Ish Shalom, p. 111a); *Shir Rabbah* 1:2; *Makkot* 24a, etc. For the view that all ten commandments were heard spoken by God, see *Mekhilta Yitro, ba-hodesh* 9 (ed. Horowitz-Rabin, p. 237).

The philosopher Franz Rosenzweig—Rosenzweig, "The Commandments: Divine or Human," included in his *On Jewish Learning*

(New York: Schocken, 1955), beginning. See the discussion by Rivka Horwitz in *Jewish Spirituality* 11, pp. 358ff.

Another radically minimalist view—Scholem, *On the Kabbalah and Its Symbolism,* pp. 29ff.

p. 118

More like the breaking down of a wall—See the text from *Otsar Ḥayyim,* quoted by Idel in KNP, p. 67 and p. 306, n. 69.

The claim is not being made for Moses alone—See *Toledot Ya'akov Yosef* 74a (on "You shall be holy"), quoted by S. Dresner, *The Zaddik* (New York: Schocken, 1974), p. 276, n. 23.

Or Akiva—A contemporary Jewish spirituality would do well to reclaim this figure of Akiva, a nonprophet who lived in "ordinary" historic time, who nevertheless "went in and came forth in peace" and had "things revealed" to him "that had not been revealed to Moses." Interestingly, of the variants on the Pardes tale (*Hagigah* 15a and parallels), some say "went and came down in peace," whereas others refer to "in" and "out." An interesting example of the interchangeability of the vertical and internal metaphors! With regard to Akiva's "journey," the Gaonic commentators are already willing to concede that he went nowhere in the "geographical" sense, but that the entire experience took place "within the chambers of his heart." We, of course, understand the "ascent" of Moses in the same way.

p. 121

Covenant is our willingness to be a channel—The image of the Jew as a channel for divine blessing into the world is widespread in Hasidism. This is the main hasidic understanding of the special role of Israel in the world, that is, the covenant.

"Israel exists"—*Zohar* 2:181b.

Is it not the God within us who chooses to hear. . . .—See *Kedushat Levi, Yitro* (ed. Jerusalem, 1958) 138b. See also the passage by Dov Baer of Myzedyrzec quoted by Rivka Schatz in *Quietistic Elements in 18th Century Hasidic Thought* (Jerusalem: Magnes, 1968), pp. 111ff. (H), as well as other sources quoted in that chapter (8). This Hebrew work is about to appear in English translation (Princeton University Press), and will make some very important materials accessible to the English reader for the first time. This book is filled with sources that run along these lines.

p. 122

But the other no less serious, and perhaps more difficult, task—I first wrote about this subject more than twenty years ago in a little essay called "Toward a Theology of Jewish Spirituality," first published in *Worship* (1971) and reprinted in J. Sleeper and A. Mintz's *The New Jews* (New York: Vintage Press, 1971). In those days, I was highly impatient—like a good 27-year-old in 1968—with the institutional side of religion.

The civilization the Jewish people creates in this active response . . . has to evolve continually—Mordecai Kaplan's evolutionary model for Jewish civilization, including both *halakhah* and *aggadah* in their fullest cultural sense, is theologically vital to me. It is quite fully integrated with my neo-kabbalistic theology. If the true core of revelation is the name of God, Torah becomes a "garment" that embodies the name. There is good kabbalistic precedent for this view (see the previous reference to Idel in *Jerusalem Studies* I, as well as the treatment of *The Secret of Garment in the Zohar,* by Dorit Cohen-Alloro, pp. 45ff.)(H). I differ from the orthodox kabbalist in my insistence that it is we Israelites who, through our love and devotion, weave even that Torah garment (and not only our own soul garments). The name is divine; the garb in which it is contained is human—divine. Therefore, the garb must evolve as humanity evolves, or else one is left with a relic, rather than an organic garment that "fits" the name of Y-H-W-H in our day. Within the framework of this commitment, I turn out to be rather a conservative on the matter of change in religious forms. More on that to follow.

p. 124

Only human . . . merely human—Cf. Rosenzweig's posing of the question: "Can we really draw so rigid a boundary between what is divine and what is human?" Compare his essay, "The Commandments: Divine or Human," quoted previously, p. 119.

p. 125

This is reflected in the language of our holiday blessings—In a lecture I heard him deliver, Rabbi J. B. Soloveichik distinguished the holiness of festivals from that of *Shabbat,* based upon the language of the blessings. *Shabbat* is sanctified directly by God from Creation, and Israel is given the privilege of joining into celebration of God's sabbath. But the holiness of the festivals is derivative from the holiness of the people Israel, since the fixing of the calendar is in their hands. Hence the mention of Israel before the festival in the festival blessings.

p. 127

In the life force—For a parallel to this understanding of divine will, see Ish-Shalom, *Ha-Rav Kook,* pp. 88ff., and sources quoted in n. 200.

p. 128

Teshuvah, **the turning of all things toward their root in God, may be seen as a reflection of divine will**—See the discussion by Meshullam Feibush Heller of Zbarash in *Likkutim Yekarim* (Jerusalem, 1974), p. 137b. This precedes, and may be a source for, the well-known views of Rav Kook, to be discussed later. On this author and his place in the history of Jewish devotional literature, see the doctoral dissertation of my student Miles Krassen (University of Pennsylvania, 1989). Krassen also offers there an important discussion of *devekut* and mystical union in the hasidic sources.

p. 129

When the Torah claims that Abraham observed God's law— Or so both Philo and the rabbis read Genesis 26:5. See my brief treatment of the Philonic materials in my *Devotion and Commandment: The Faith of Abraham in the Hasidic Imagination,* pp. 24ff., and the sources quoted there.

p. 130

These universal moral commandments are incumbent upon all human individuals—On the Noahide laws and their implications, see David Novak, *The Image of the Non-Jew in Judaism: An Historical and Constructive Study of the Noahide Laws* (New York: Edward Mellen Press, 1983).

p. 133

"Negate your will before God's will"—*Avot* 2:4.

p. 135

Brit ha-lashon, "the covenant of the tongue"—The phrase goes back to *Sefer Yetsirah,* which sees this covenant and that of the flesh or sexuality *(brit ha-ma'or)* juxtaposed to one another. Speech and sexuality are parallel areas of human expression; both need to be guarded by covenantal purity.

p. 136

We now take that same language—See my introduction to *Your Word Is Fire,* as well as several of the texts in that volume that speak of verbal prayer as a return of the divine gift of speech in Torah.

p. 140

When Israel arrived at the mountain . . ., they encamped there "with a single heart"—*Mekhilta Yitro, ba-ḥodesh* 1, p. 206; RaSHI to Exodus 19:2.

p. 142

Loss of our distinctive Jewish identity—The rabbis say that Israel were redeemed from Egypt because they kept their distinctive Jewish names, maintained the Hebrew language, did not betray their secrets, etc. For the various versions of this list see *Va-Yikra Rabbah* 32:5 and parallels.

The exile of the mind . . . the exile of language—These terms are commonly found in the literature of early Hasidism, and are employed to spell out the hasidic spiritual interpretation of the Exodus from Egypt. Mine is an updated version of that hasidic reading.

p. 143

According to one hasidic view—This is the text from *Kedushat Levi,* by Levi Yizhak of Berdichev, that I translated for B. W. Holtz's *Back to the Sources* (New York: Summit, 1984), pp. 361ff.

p. 144

The "handmaiden at the sea"—*Mekhilta beshalaḥ, shirta* 3, p. 126.

p. 147

Revelation is not a one time event, but an ongoing process—
See Scholem's treatment of this theme in "Revelation and Tradition
as Religious Categories in Judaism" in his *The Messianic Idea in
Judaism* (New York: Schocken, 1971), pp. 282ff., and especially the
kabbalistic sources quoted on pp. 298ff. In the past, recognition of
the ongoing quality of revelation was largely, though not wholly,
limited to the revelation of the divine will in the halakhic decision-
making process. I would seek to conceive it in somewhat broader
terms, embracing *aggadah* and religious creativity, as well.

"A great voice that never ceased"—Deuteronomy 5:19.

Redemption

p. 154

The light that came forth was too bright—*Bereshit Rabbah* 11:2;
12:6.

Our task is to bring the sparks together—On the uplifting of
sparks as a theme in Jewish mystical literature, see the treatment by
Louis Jacobs in *Jewish Spirituality* II.

p. 157

But we know a deeper truth as well—Here, I have in mind the
distinction between "truth" and "truth of truth," as discussed by
Nahman of Bratslav in *Likkutey MoHaRaN* 64. See my translation

and discussion in *Tormented Master,* pp. 311ff. This teaching by Nahman is a key passage for any Jewish treatment of theodicy.

p. 159

"The king has brought me into His chambers"—Song of Songs 1:4.

p. 160

There is only one city—See M. Idel, *Jerusalem in Medieval Jewish Thought,* and especially the comments by Y. Liebes in "De Natura Dei: On the Development of Jewish Myth," part 4, n. 14, in his forthcoming SUNY volume on Jewish myth, *Myth & Messianism in Jewish History.*

"For My house shall be called . . ."—Isaiah 56:7.

p. 161

"Return to Me and I shall return to you"—Malachi 3:7.

p. 163

Knowledge and life became two trees—See the sources quoted and discussion by G. Scholem in "Sitra Ahra: Good and Evil in the Kabbalah" in his *On the Mystical Shape of the Godhead.* See also N. N. Glatzer, "Franz Kafka and the Tree of Knowledge" (in his *Essays in Jewish Thought;* University, Alabama: University of Alabama Press, 1978; pp. 184ff.), referring to treatment of this theme in Kafka's *Parables and Paradoxes* (New York: Schocken, 1946). Kafka's insights are a surprising parallel to those of the medieval kabbalists. For an even earlier reference, see *Midrash Aggadah* (ed. S. Buber, p. 6), *Bereshit,* which notes that "the blessed Holy One did not say: 'Tree of Knowledge,' but rather Moses, who wrote the Torah, called it the Tree of Knowledge. Neither did Adam know it was the Tree of Knowledge, nor did Eve, who said to the snake: 'Of the tree that is in the center of the garden' and did not say: 'the Tree of Knowledge.' " This is a remarkable text for several reasons. See also the parallel in *Midrash Tadshe* (Jellinek, *Bet ha-Midrash* 3:169).

p. 164

Into the hands of Torah—I understand "Torah" here as the ongoing process of reading and interpretation, of making Torah's tales ours and using them to tell and amplify our own. The ongoing relationship between the fixed text and the ever-changing generations and their need to reinterpret becomes the lifeblood of Judaism. In this understanding of Torah, I have been much influenced by the early hasidic masters, who speak frequently of the need to read Torah anew in accord with the spirit of each generation. They were able to do this without emptying the ancient vessel of its own content. On the interpretive process and its key place in Judaism, see the important essay "On Interpretation," by S. Rawidowicz, in his *Studies in Jewish Thought* (Philadelphia: Jewish Publication Society, 1974), pp. 45ff. That essay, along with Scholem's "Revelation and Tradition," to which I have referred earlier, has been crucial to the development of my own thinking on these questions.

Then the Garden had to be protected—See Kafka, *Parables and Paradoxes,* p. 29: "In a sense our expulsion from Paradise was a stroke of luck, for had we not been expelled, Paradise would have had to be destroyed."

p. 165

"Every place where Israel were exiled . . ."—*Megillah* 29a and parallels. See the discussion of the *Shekhinah's* exile by Heschel in *Torah min ha-Shamayim* I, pp. 68ff.

The exile of Israel . . . is thus uplifted and transformed—See Scholem's "Kabbalah and Myth" in *On the Kabbalah and Its Symbolism*, pp. 115ff., and Tishby's discussion of *Galut Shekhinah* in *Wisdom*, vol. 1, pp. 382ff, 409ff.

p. 167

Thus far the Book of Genesis—For this reading, I am indebted to my friend Arnold Eisen. Cf. his *Galut: Modern Jewish Reflections on Homelessness and Homecoming* (Bloomington IN: Indiana University Press, 1986).

p. 168

"The mountain of Y-H-W-H's house. . . ."—Micah 4:1.

p. 169

Homecoming and *Teshuvah*—This reading of *teshuvah* is influenced by that of Rav Kook. See his "Lights of Penitence" in *Abraham Isaac Kook: The Lights of Penitence, Lights of Holiness, Moral Principles, Essays, Lectures, and Poems,* Ben Zion Bokser, ed., and the work by B. Ish-Shalom, to which I have referred earlier. Ish-Shalom also discusses the Western (Bergson et al.) as well as the earlier kabbalistic influences on Kook's thought.

p. 170

Teshuvah* to *binah—See Tishby, *Wisdom* vol. 3, pp. 1501ff.

p. 171

"I am my beloved's"—Song of Songs 6:3. ELUL is taken to be an acronym for this phrase.

p. 172

The rabbis claim—The following discussion is influenced by several passages in *Sefat Emet,* where much emphasis is placed upon this rabbinic reading of the Yamim Nora'im and their meaning.

The occasion when Moses cries out—Exodus 34.

p. 173

"The tablets were of God's workmanship. . . ."—Exodus 32:16.

"Carve yourself two tablets. . . ."—Exodus 34:1.

p. 174

"As You have borne. . . ."—Numbers 14:19.

According to one old interpretation—I have heard this interpretation quoted in the name of R. Isaiah Horowitz, but I have not been able to find it in his writings.

p. 177

The saving of God—For the rabbinic background to this phrase, see Heschel, *Torah min ha-Shamayim,* I, pp. 65ff. The idea that God is the object as well as the subject of redemption was seen as a daring assertion in rabbinic times, a threat to the notion of divine omnipotence. Such passages were thus ignored by the philosophic rereading of rabbinic Judaism that dominated in the early medieval world and again in the nineteenth- and early twentieth-century West. But they were the very heart of rabbinic tradition as understood by the kabbalists. Their image of Y-H-W-H was one deeply colored by the metaphor of cosmic exile and the divine need for restoration. This restoration of divine wholeness could only be effected by the human deed. It is this Jewish theology, I am suggesting, that needs to serve as the basis for our thinking about God in the post-Holocaust and postmodern age.

p. 179

Torah, worship, and acts of compassion—*Avot* 1:2.

p. 181

"To establish this world as God's kingdom"—I intentionally quote the whole phrase from the *alenu* prayer. The phrase *tikkun olam* is bandied about a good bit these days, but too often separated from *be-malkhut Shaddai*. There is *everything worldly, but nothing secular,* about this value of the Jewish tradition.

p. 182

A chaos of messianic dreams—The primary collection of these is in the Talmud, *Sanhedrin* 97–99. The jumbled character is immediately apparent there.

p. 184

The kabbalistic myth of creation—See Scholem, *Major Trends in Jewish Mysticism,* pp. 260ff., and at greater length in "Schoepfung aus Nichts und Selbstverschraenkung Gottes," *Eranos Jahrbuch* 25 (1956).

GLOSSARY

Adonay—Literally: My Lord. Used as a euphemism to avoid oral or written mention of Y-H-W-H.

Aggadah—Literally: Narrative. Nonlegal portions of rabbinic literature, including homilies, legends, theology, etc.

Ahavat ha-Briot—Love of fellow humans, or, taken literally, fellow creatures.

Ahavat Yisrael—Love for one's fellow Jews.

Ayin—Literally: Nothing. The inner no-thing of divinity, out of which all being flows; hence the true core of existence. The designation of being as ayin in fact reflects the first stage in its journey toward definition. See Eyn Sof.

Barukh Shem—Opening words of the formula "Blessed is the name of God's glorious kingdom for ever and ever!" recited in the ancient Temple in response to hearing the pronunciation of the Name, and still found in Jewish worship, immediately following the *Sh'ma.*

Benschen—Literally: Blessing (Yiddish). Refers especially to the blessing after meals.

Beyn Adam le-Ḥavero—Between fellow persons. Refers to those of the commandments that govern the interpersonal and social realm, as distinct from those that are purely *beyn Adam le-Makom,* between the person and God.

Binah—Literally: Understanding. The third of the ten *sefirot.* Often described in maternal terms, *binah* is the womb out of which the seven lower manifestations are born or the fountain out of which they flow. *Binah* is also the object of *teshuvah,* the source to which all life returns.

Brit—Covenant. Often used to refer specifically to the covenant of Abraham or circumcision.

Brit ha-Lashon—Covenant of the tongue. Refers to the covenant of Sinai, in which the Word or speech plays the central role.

Da'at—Literally: Knowledge. Often better translated as "awareness," in some kabbalistic systems *da'at* serves as the synthesis of *ḥokhmah* and *binah,* completing the highest or intellectual triad of *sefirot.*

Davar, devarim—Word, words. Also used to mean "things."

Daven—Pray (Yiddish), especially to chant liturgical prayers in the style of traditionally pious Jews.

Elohim—The generic Hebrew term for God or gods. The noun retains its ancient plural form, but is used with singular verbs when referring to the God of Israel.

Erets Yisra'el—The Land of Israel.

Eyn Sof—Literally: The Endless. The primal undefined Godhead, out of which both the *sefirot* and world emerge. A totality of being even more recondite than *ayin,* not yet definable even as having entered into the passageway of no-thing that will lead toward being.

Ezer ke-Negdo—The relationship of Eve to Adam, as in Genesis 2:20. Usually translated "helpmate," but more literally "a help over against him."

Halakhah—Literally: The Path or the Walking. The system of Jewish religious praxis as codified in sacred law.

Havurah—Fellowship. An intimate community of Jews who share in study, prayer, and an understanding of the religious life.

Hiyyut—The life-force; divine energy as manifest in God's creatures.

Hol—Profane, ordinary. Distinguished from *kodesh,* the holy.

Kashrut—Literally: fitness. Usually refers to fitness for consumption according to the *halakhah* of permitted and forbidden foods.

Kavvanah—Inner direction or concentration, particularly in prayer.

Keva—Literally: Fixedness. Refers to the set forms of devotion, like the fixed text of the liturgy. Stands in creative tension with *kavvanah.*

Kiddush—Literally: Sanctification. The proclamation of the Sabbath or festival, generally recited over a raised cup of wine.

Kiddush ha-Shem—Literally: Sanctification of the Name. A public act that proclaims God's glory. Includes, but is not limited to, acts of martyrdom.

Kiddushin—The act of marriage, or the Jewish marriage.

Klal Yisrael—The entirety of the Jewish people.

Le-Shem Yihud—Literally: For the sake of unification. An introductory formula recited by kabbalists and others before the fulfillment of a mitsvah, indicating the intent of uniting the primal pair of Blessed Holy One and *Shekhinah* by means of that deed.

Leshon ha-Kodesh—The holy tongue. The Hebrew language, but by extension used to refer to purity of speech.

Medabber—Literally: Speaker. The designation of human, as distinct from other forms of being, in classical Hebrew speech.

Memale—Ellipse for *memale kulho almin,* "filling all the worlds," a kabbalistic designation for divinity as immanence.

Metsavah—Commander; the One who stands as the voice of authority behind the *mitsvot.*

Mezuzah—Literally: Doorpost. The small oblong container attached to the doorposts of Jewish homes, containing a parchment that bears the words of the *Sh'ma.*

Middat ha-Din—The attribute of judgment, paired in rabbinic writings with *middat ha-rahamim,* the attribute of mercy, the two primal qualities God is said to keep in balance when relating to the human community.

Mitsvah, mitsvot—Commandments; prescriptions and proscriptions of the Torah.

Moshe Rabbenu—Moses our Teacher.

Raki'a—Sky; in ancient Hebrew myth, the disk into which the stars and luminaries are fixed.

Reshut ha-Yahid—Literally: Private domain. Term used particularly in connection with Sabbath law. By extension in kabbalistic language: the domain of the One.

Ruah kol basar—The spirit of all flesh. A phrase from the Sabbath morning service.

Sefirah, Sefirot—According to the kabbalists, the ten stages by which divinity is manifest, as well as the ten rungs to be traversed and unified in the return to the One.

Shaharit—The daily morning service, to be recited at dawn.

Shalosh Regalim—The three pilgrimage festivals: Pesah, Shavu'ot, Sukkot.

Shekhinah—Literally: Indwelling. The tenth *sefirah*; the aspect of divinity most associated with the feminine, receiving and absorbing the qualities of the other *sefirot* as the moon absorbs and reflects sunlight, or like the sea into which all rivers flow. *Shekhinah* is divinity as manifest within this world.

Shem ha-Meforash—The explicit name Y-H-W-H. The term may also refer to more extended esoteric names of God.

Sh'ma; Sh'ma Yisrael—Hear O Israel! The essential watchword of Jewish faith, found in Deuteronomy 6:4ff. and recited twice daily as the centerpiece of Jewish worship.

Shtetl—Town (Yiddish). The typically Jewish small or medium-sized town where most Jews in Eastern Europe lived until the turn of the twentieth century.

Sovev—Ellipse for *sovev kulho almin,* surrounding all the worlds; in kabbalistic language, God as beyond or outside the universe. Paired with *memale.*

Tefillin—Phylacteries; holy boxes containing biblical passages, worn by Jews during weekday morning prayers.

Teshuvah—Return to God; repentance.

Tikkun—Repair; restoration. Refers especially to the restoration of the cosmos through the regimen of the *mitsvot.*

Tsa'ar Ba'aley Ḥayyim—Literally: The Pain of Living Creatures. A moral concern that calls for avoidance of all unnecessary pain or cruelty to animals.

Tsaddik—Literally: Just One. The Jewish Holy Person; the one who fulfills the ideals of Jewish piety.

Tselem Elohim—The image of God.

Tsimtsum—The contraction or concentration of divinity. A key concept in Jewish mystical theories of Creation; the act by which God allowed "room" for the world or the separate human psyche to exist.

Yesh me-Ayin—Creation out of nothing. The doctrine that God created the world without reference to prime matter or preexistent essences.

Yiḥud—Union, unification. Used in mystical parlance, but also refers to marital union.

Yiḥud ha-Shem—Unification of the Name. Proclamation of divine unity or the living out of deeds that make God's unity a reality.

INDEX

About the Author

Arthur (Avraham Yizhak) Green teaches at the Reconstructionist Rabbinical College, where he also serves as college president. He is a student of Jewish mysticism and Hasidism, combining a historical approach to those sources with a search for their meaning to contemporary Jews. He is author of *Tormented Master: A Life of Rabbi Nahman of Bratslav,* editor of *Jewish Spirituality,* and translator of several collections of Hasidic teachings. The present volume, his first work on contemporary theology, is a distillation of many years of study and teaching.